EVE
SPOKE

EVE SPOKE

HUMAN LANGUAGE AND

HUMAN EVOLUTION

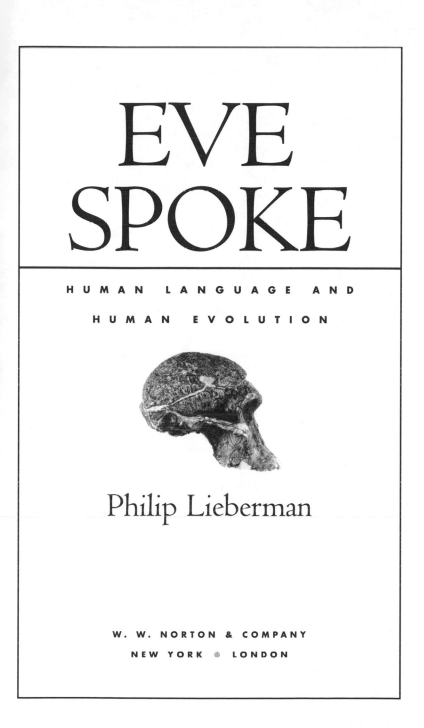

Philip Lieberman

W. W. NORTON & COMPANY

NEW YORK ● LONDON

For information about permission to reproduce selections from
this book, write to Permissions, W. W. Norton & Company, Inc.,
500 Fifth Avenue, New York, NY 10110.

The text of this book is composed in Bembo
with the display set in Futura
Desktop composition by Tom Ernst
Manufacturing by Quebecor Printing, Fairfield Inc.
Book designed by Judith Stagnitto Abbate

Library of Congress Cataloging-in-Publication Data

Lieberman, Philip.
Eve spoke : human language and human evolution / Philip
Lieberman.
p.   cm.
Includes bibliographical references and index.
ISBN 0-393-04089-5
1. Language and languages—Origin. 2. Human evolution.
3. Behavior evolution. I. Title.
P116.L53   1998
401—dc21
97-17100
CIP

W. W. Norton & Company, Inc., 500 Fifth Avenue,
New York, NY 10110
http://www.wwnorton.com

W. W. Norton & Company Ltd., 10 Coptic Street, London
WC1A 1PU

1 2 3 4 5 6 7 8 9 0

In remembrance: Ben, Harry, Minna, and Miriam

Contents

Acknowledgments

In relating a research project that has spanned thirty years, I find it almost impossible to remember all the contributions and insightful comments of my colleagues, students, and critics. Some of the people whose aid I most readily recall are Edmund Crelin, with whom I worked when he made the first reconstructions of fossil hominid vocal tracts. Dennis Klatt and I then worked together on the modeling of the reconstructed vocal tracts to determine their speech limitations. Jeffrey Laitman continued the vocal tract reconstruction project. Franklin Cooper, Alvin Liberman, Leigh Lisker, Katherine Harris, and Arthur Abramson made Haskins Laboratories a stimulating center of research. Kenneth Stevens, Arthur House, and Terrance Nearey provided major insights on the nature of speech perception and production. In the recent past, Sheila Blumstein, Peter Eimas, John Donoghue, Emily Pickett, Thanassi Protopappas, W. Techumseh Fitch, and, most especially, Joseph Friedman have made major contributions to my attempts to understand how brains work. And Daniel Lieberman's careful reading of major portions of this book was crucial, as are his contributions to an ongoing reappraisal of Neanderthal vocal tract anatomy and the general principles by which evolution shapes the skull. Patricia Schreiber's illustrations grace the book. Finally, Drake McFeely and Angela von der Lippe patiently read and reread the text and made cogent comments thereon. To all, I offer my thanks.

Preface

I Talk, Therefore I Am

Put less cryptically, this book is about how we came to be; part of the answer is that speech and language shaped the evolution of our immediate ancestors, the first modern human beings. About 150,000 years ago, "modern" human beings appeared in Africa and the Mideast. These were people who had the tongues and mouths and, most important, the brain mechanisms that allow us to produce articulate speech and express complex thoughts. The superior brains of our ancestors, not their brawn, allowed them to displace the archaic human beings, the Neanderthal and *Homo erectus* populations, whom they encountered as they moved across Europe and Asia and to Australia. In short, Eve and Adam and their progeny prevailed because they talked.

I will in the pages that follow try to show that our ability to talk is one of the keys to understanding the evolutionary process that made us human. Human speech in itself is a distinct human attribute. It's clear that human beings are not stronger or more adaptable than other, competing species. Horses run faster, gorillas are stronger, bacteria adapt faster to different environments. Speech, language, and thought differentiate humans from other species. The premise of this book is that these distinctive human qualities are biologically linked; neural mechanisms adapted for regulating speech production appear to be implicated in recalling the meaning of a word and in comprehending the meaning of a sentence. Parts of the brain that regulate speech production also appear to make abstract thought possible. The case is not water-tight; there are many loose ends and unanswered questions. Many years of research will be necessary for us to understand how the human brain works. But I am convinced and will try to show that the evolutionary process that formed the brain mechanisms that allow us to talk produced the *human* brain, a brain adapted for thought and language that differentiates humans from all other liv-ing species.

Inferences concerning prehistory, like other theories, are really informed guesses that are then tested against "scientific" evidence. So this book is also a sort of detective story, the story of why and how we can guess that particular events actually occurred. Much of the scientific evidence that I'll try to explain is new and isn't familiar to the general public or, for that matter, to most profes-sional anthropologists, archaeologists, or linguists. We humans seem to have evolved a special-purpose "language-thinking system" that allows us to think in abstract terms and rapidly communicate our thoughts to other people. The evolution of this system, which entailed the restructuring of anatomy originally adapted for eating, breathing, and making a limited number of sounds and modifica-tions to the brain (which still are not understood), involved the same Darwinian mechanisms that produced the distinctive attri-butes of other animals, such as the elephant's trunk and the tiger's stripes. But the end result of our particular distinctive evolutionary process was a capacity for thinking that had never existed before and that has changed the world to a form that also had never existed before.

Many of the techniques that have, in the past decade, revealed the nature of the human language-thinking system did not exist earlier. Techniques such as positron emission tomography (PET), magnetic resonance imaging (MRI), and functional magnetic resonance imaging (FMRI) allow us to view the structure of living brains and make reasonable inferences about the way they work. Tracer techniques have revealed some of the complex pathways of the brain. Computer systems that generate and analyze speech have shown that human vocal communication is a key element that makes it possible for us to transmit complex thoughts to each other at rates unattainable by other means. Producing human speech likewise involves our ability to perform acrobatic maneuvers with our tongues, lips, and larynx, controlled by brain mechanisms that don't exist in any other living species. I'll attempt to convey the essential nature of these techniques without becoming mired in technobabble and to show how these findings relate to other exciting discoveries, such as Jane Goodall's observations of chimpanzees and their linguistic abilities, what human infants perceive, and the comparative, archaeological, and fossil studies that have enlightened our understanding of how we came to be.

I'll also necessarily have to enter some of the current scientific debates on human evolution and the neural underpinnings of human language. The "multiregional" theory of human evolution claims that modern humans evolved locally in different places and times from resident archaic populations. Milford Wolpoff of the University of Michigan, Fred Smith of the University of Tennessee, and other exponents of this theory often claim that there is no real functional distinction between modern human beings and Neanderthals, and that Neanderthals spoke as we do. Being at the center of the Neanderthal speech storm, I won't be taking a neutral position; I think the evidence shows that Neanderthals were very, very different from any living human beings. The Eve hypothesis is most likely correct; we are the descendants of an Eve and an Adam, who most likely spoke and thought as we do. Noam Chomsky's theories concerning human language and the organization of the human brain also fail to fit with these new insights into the nature and evolution of the biological bases of human language. I will discuss some of Chomsky's claims and present data that refute them. His basic premise, that the central characteristics of language, one of the most complex aspects of human behavior, are strictly determined by our genes, is part of a trend. The claim that human moral conduct results from a "morality gene" is also without merit.

It is worth mentioning, too, that not everything about the evolution of human beings, language, and thought is deadly serious. By reading further, you'll be able to explain why dogs snarl, why boys purse their lips but girls smile when they talk, and how your friends might fare should they plan to climb Mount Everest.

EVE
SPOKE

CHAPTER 1

The Mice
Talked at Night

THE SKY WAS nearer black than blue. At 24,000 feet on Mount Everest, Dr. Mike keyed his radio and began to speak. Far below at the Khumbu Glacier Base Camp, I punched the record button of the digital tape recorder connected to my Motorola Maxtrax two-way radio. We were testing my evolutionary theory that the brain mechanisms that control our tongues, larynx, and lips when we talk are the evolutionary bases for complex human thought. The experiment was successful. As we reported in *Nature*, the international journal of science, the climbing teams' speech motor control and their ability to comprehend simple sentences had both deteriorated.[1] By the time they had reached 24,000 feet, they needed 50 percent more time to understand sentences that six-year-old children readily comprehend. The lack of oxygen at extreme altitudes affected brain mechanisms that regulate both speech motor control and syntax. The climbers' decision-making abilities deteriorated as well. Putting these effects together with the results of many other independent experimental studies, we were able to show that the parts of the human brain that control speech also play a part in thinking.

Over the past thirty years my colleagues and I have studied monkeys, chimpanzees, infants, children, normal adults, dyslexic adults, elderly people, and patients suffering from Parkinson's disease and other types of brain damage. We have also examined the skulls of our fossil ancestors, comparing them with those of newborn infants and apes. The focus of these studies has been the puzzle surrounding human evolution. Why are we so different from other animals, although we are at the same time so similar?

Anatomists have for centuries known that we share many features with our nearest animal "cousin"—the chimpanzee. Modern biology has only deepened the mystery. In terms of the genetic information encoded in the DNA sequences that determine the structure of their bodies, human beings and chimpanzees are more similar to each other than rabbits and hares are to each other. Every new fossil discovery confirms the fact that our not-so-distant ancestors, the various australopithecine species, resembled chimpanzees four or five million years ago, an instant in the flow of time. Why, then, are we humans so different from all other living creatures, and how could this have come to pass? Part of the answer seems to be that we are able to think because we can talk. Brain structures originally designed to control our tongues and lips, as well as our hands, may have become modified and elaborated for language and thinking.

In some deep, unconscious way we "know" that dogs, cats, chimpanzees, and other intelligent animals would be human if they could only talk. Intuitively we know that talking = thinking = being human. The studies discussed below show that this intuition is correct. We know, so far as science "knows" anything, that speech is a central aspect of human language. Speech consists of more than a set of arbitrary sounds that people can use to communicate. The particular acoustic properties of human speech allow us to transmit information rapidly to each other. The complex ballet constantly performed by the muscles of our speech anatomy—our lips, tongue, vocal cords, and so on—is choreographed by specialized brain mechanisms that also appear to make complex human thought possible. The fossil record of human evolution and genetic evidence show that these brain mechanisms and anatomy reached their present state fairly recently. We, *Homo sapiens loquax*, evolved in the last 150,000 years or so, most likely in Africa, from which we spread out and populated the world, displacing earlier human-like animals.

Indeed, these prehistoric events may be dimly reflected in the mythology that forms our human heritage. The Popol Vuh, the Mayan story of creation, for example, links being able to talk with being human:

> Having created all the birds and animals, the creators said to them: Talk and scream according to your kind, pronounce and praise our name, say that we are your Fathers and Mothers, as we are indeed. Speak, praise, invoke us.
>
> But even though this was commanded of them, they could not speak as humans, they only screamed, cackled and hissed. They tried to put words together and hail the creator, they were punished and since then their meat has been eaten by man.

The Gospel according to John is even more direct:

> In the beginning was the Word, and the Word was with God, and the Word was God.

And as Beatrix Potter knew, in the small hours of the night the mice met to talk to each other. Speech is so essential to our concept of intelligence that its possession is virtually equated with being human. Animals who talk *are* human, because what sets us apart from other animals is the "gift" of speech.

Eve and the Neanderthals

Although the speech ability of the Neanderthals who lived in Europe and Asia forty thousand years ago and the brain mechanisms controlling speech and thinking seem to be unlikely topics for acrimonious dispute, barrels of printer's ink have been spilled in this controversy and countless harsh words uttered. The evolutionary and biological natures of human speech and language directly impinge on two issues. One contentious issue is how human beings evolved. The speech deficiencies of the "classic" European Neanderthals are consistent with the Eve hypothesis— that modern human beings evolved in Africa some 150,000 years ago and then migrated to Europe, Asia, and Australia, displacing the archaic humanlike hominids who had reached these areas in an earlier wave of hominid expansion. All contemporary human beings, therefore, have common African ancestors, according to the Eve theory, and no present human population is directly related to the Neanderthals. The opposing "multiregional" theory of human evolution holds that modern human beings evolved locally in different places and times. According to the multiregional theory, native Asians, Africans, Australians, and Europeans independently evolved in these locales from resident *Homo erectus* populations that had emigrated there from Africa about one million years ago. Milford Wolpoff of the University of Michigan is perhaps its foremost proponent.

The multiregional theory is beset by many problems. It is based on the premise that the small differences in skull shape and other bones that differentiate the teeth and skulls of contemporary Asians supposedly were similar to those of *Homo erectus* who lived in Asia because Asian *Homo sapiens* supposedly evolved from these extinct hominids. Contemporary Europeans supposedly evolved from European Neanderthals, who, in turn, differed from Asian *Homo erectus*, who, in turn, differed from a hypothetical Australian *Homo erectus* population. But if that were the case, we would have to account for the fact that all living human beings are remarkably similar. If we independently evolved, why are central human characteristics—our brains, anatomy, and physiology—so similar throughout the world? Any normal human child can effortlessly acquire any human language before the age of three years. Antibiotics work, subject to similar individual variations, in similar fashion in all parts of the world. An unlikely explanation has been offered by multiregionalist theorists who propose that "gene flow" occurred after the independent evolution of different human groups. However, if the extensive mating of these populations necessary to yield similar basic human attributes happened after the hypothetical independent evolution from *Homo erectus*, why would small regional distinctions survive unless they were really adaptive? In this case, the Eve hypothesis also can account for adaptive regional differences.

Moreover, the skeletal comparisons cited by Milford Wolpoff and his colleagues are suspect. Neanderthals, for example, are very different from any modern humans; they are extinct. William W. Howells, working at the Peabody Museum of Anthropology and Ethnology of Harvard University, has spent decades studying the skulls of human populations throughout the world. He has demonstrated that Neanderthal skulls have characteristics that never occur in modern human beings; modern human beings, conversely, have features that never occur in Neanderthals. In fact, the specific skeletal "evidence" cited by multiregionalists to support their theory appears to be irrelevant. A collaborative study (Frayer et al.) that was supposed to clinch the case for the multiregional argument, presented in 1993 the list of skeletal features supposedly linking modern Asians, Europeans, and Australians to the *Homo erectus* and Neanderthal fossils found in Asia, Europe, and Australia. However, Daniel Lieberman, who is now at Rutgers University, two years later showed that most of these supposedly diagnostic features do not bear on the debate. Some of them, such as the shape of the incisor teeth, were found to a greater or lesser degree in all archaic fossil hominids and modern humans throughout the world. These features, therefore, cannot be used to link contemporary human beings who lived in a particular part of the world to *Homo erectus* populations that previously lived there. Other features, such as larger jawbones, were affected by environmental factors. A larger jawbone is not entirely specified by a person's genes; it can result anywhere when a person chews harder and more often. Daniel Lieberman, who is also "my son the anthropologist," demonstrated that the remaining skeletal features cited by Frayer and his colleagues supported the Eve hypothesis.

The reason that Neanderthal speech is a central issue in the debate concerning the Eve hypothesis is that people tend to have children with mates who speak the same language or dialect. Recent studies show beyond any reasonable doubt that speech serves as a genetic isolating mechanism in modern human beings. Therefore, the speech differences that my colleagues and I believe existed between Neanderthals and early modern human beings could have kept them apart for many generations. The Neanderthal–human speech distinction takes on significance since the demographic model developed by Ezra Zubrow of the State University of New York at Buffalo shows that Neanderthals would gradually have become extinct over many generations if their early modern human competitors had possessed only slight advantages. Zubrow's model is consistent with the archaeological record (discussed in Chapter 4), which shows that most of the stone tools of early modern human beings were similar to those of contemporary Neanderthals for tens of thousands of years. The gradual-extinction model is also consistent with the reappraisal of Neanderthal speech capabilities that will be presented here; Neanderthals clearly possessed language and speech, but their speech capabilities were intermediate between those of still earlier hominids and those of modern humans. Neanderthal speech would immediately have been perceived as being different from that of our ancestors. We therefore do not have to script a blitzkrieg in which modern human beings, our ancestors, overwhelmed the Neanderthals because they were ten times smarter or could talk ten times faster.

In short, we can account for the extinction of the Neanderthals if modern humans possessed only slight advantages, providing that the populations were genetically isolated. If Neanderthal and early human groups acted as we do, and kept apart because of speech differences, then small cognitive and linguistic advantages acting over many generations would have resulted in human beings gradually replacing Neanderthals. Given the role of speech as an isolating mechanism, exponents of the multi-regional theory who claim that Neanderthals and modern humans mated must also claim that Neanderthal speech capabilities did not differ from those of modern human beings.[2]

Noam Chomsky's Linguistic Theories

The other scientific debate that we'll consider involves Noam Chomsky's linguistic theories. In Eleanor Lattimore's account of the wild "honeymoon" trip that she and her husband, Owen,[3] made in the 1930s across Central Asia from Soviet Siberia through wild bandit-infested regions of China, across the Himalayan mountain passes to Ladakh, she tells how local tribesmen regarded Owen as a sage. In one remote hamlet,

> other guests had arrived, two Tatars in Russian blouses and two Chantos in skull caps and loose white coats. One of the latter delighted us particularly, a fat fellow who looked like a perspiring egg with a little black skull cap on one side of his small end and his clothes hanging on him like Humpty Dumpty and always coming unbuttoned. He was avid for information of the world and spent the day mopping his face and plying Owen with questions. In fact they all sat around all day on gay rugs and asked Owen questions as if he were an oracle, one of the best of which was, "If sheep in one part of the world make the same kind of noises as sheep in any other part of the world, why is it that men don't talk the same all over the world?" (Lattimore 1934, 116–17)

All human languages use words and some form of syntax to convey distinctions of meaning. The "rules" of syntax in English, for example, convey the fact that *Mary* is the person being kissed in the sentence "Bill kissed Mary" and that she isn't the person being kissed in the sentence "Bill kissed Jane while Mary watched them."

In both cases *Bill* is the person who carries out the action. *Mary* and *Jane* are respectively the recipients of the action. It's clear that different human languages use various methods to indicate these relationships. The syntax of languages that diverged from a common ancestral language in the last few thousand years, such as English and Latin, differ dramatically. English, for instance, conveys different meanings to a limited degree using "morphemes" added to the end of a word that indicate whether a noun is plural rather than singular or whether a verb is in the past tense or not (*books* versus *book*, *walked* versus *walk*). But Latin makes greater use of morphemes to convey distinctions in meaning; the subject and object relationships conveyed by word order in English are, for example, conveyed by morphemes added to each word in Latin. A Latin-speaking child had to acquire a strategy different from that of an English-speaking child to understand the meaning of a sentence. The question arises, Why are human languages so different and how do children learn to speak and understand any language?

An obvious answer is that children learn the words and rules of syntax of their native language in much the same way that they learn everything else, by means of general cognitive processes. Although affinities can be seen in the words of many distantly related languages, such as English and Hindi, which both derive from a common ancestral language, Indo-European, their syntactic rules differ profoundly. Many aspects of the cultures of India, England, and the United States also differ, but it is evident that the specific habits and attitudes of these different cultures are learned by children as they grow up in a particular locale. Similar distinctions hold for very closely related languages and cultures, such as German and English. However, Noam Chomsky, arguably the most influential living linguist, has turned the linguistic world upside down. Chomsky claims that human beings do not really learn the rules of syntax. He instead proposes that we come equipped at birth with a "language organ" that specifies all the rules of syntax of all human languages. Chomsky's disciples (some of his leading advocates often refer to the theory as a worldwide religion) believe that a "universal grammar" is genetically coded into every human brain. The principles of the universal grammar are designed to guide every child to the "correct" set of syntax rules of any language that the child happens to hear. The hypothetical genetically coded universal grammar is identical for all human beings. These premises would be amazing if they were true.

Chomsky once categorically stated that human language couldn't have evolved by means of the processes that Charles Darwin proposed in his modestly entitled book *On the Origin of Species*. Chomsky has recently retreated from that stance, but we will see that his version of the biology and evolution of human linguistic ability is not consistent with the general principles of evolutionary biology and the studies of the brain bases of language and speech that we'll discuss.

What Makes Speech Useful?

Curiously, the property that makes human speech an essential component of language and thinking was discovered by chance. In theory, the relationship between science and engineering is that scientists discover "laws" of nature, which engineers later apply to solve practical problems. That's often the case. Albert Einstein's discovery that $E = mc^2$ preceded the nuclear age by almost forty years. However, research directed toward an engineering project showed linguists that human speech communication is a complex process by which we can effortlessly transmit information at least five times faster than by any other sounds. The following experiment that you can perform without any equipment other than a pencil, or any object that you care to tap on a table, will show you what the development group at Haskins Laboratories, which was then located in New York City, discovered in the late 1950s.

EXPERIMENT 1

1. Place the pencil in your hand and tap it on the table. Start with a slow tapping rate and gradually increase the rate, count-

ing the number of taps that you can distinctly hear in one second. Ready? Start!

2. What was the maximum tap rate?

3. Now simply talk slowly for a few seconds and try to remember what you said. Keep track of the elapsed time and write down the words that you said. Try talking fast. Calculate the number of sounds (roughly the letters of the alphabet) that you uttered (a graceless but useful word) in one second.

What you'll discover is that it's almost impossible even to differentiate and count more than seven or so taps per second. In fact, when sounds are presented at a rate that exceeds fifteen per second, they merge into a continuous buzz. However, you can easily differentiate and *identify* more than ten speech sounds per second when you talk slowly. If you talk rapidly, the maximum rate at which speech sounds can be produced and comprehended is about twenty-five to thirty sounds per second. The Haskins Laboratories team, directed by the psychologist Alvin Liberman, the physicist Franklin S. Cooper, and the linguist Pierre DeLattre, was trying to build a machine that would "read" books aloud to blind people. Computer systems that would identify printed characters were available, but artificial speech-producing systems were in the infant stage of development and generated incomprehensible noises. The solution seemed to be to use a system of non-speech sound codes for the letters that the print scanner identified. The letter *a* could, for example, be signaled by a low-pitched tone, *e* by a high-pitched tone, and so on. Traditional Morse code could also be used. However, it soon became apparent that the maximum rate at which the text could be transmitted was so slow that "readers" usually forgot the beginning of a sentence before coming to its end. Moreover, people listening to the reading machine had to concentrate intently on identifying the sounds themselves, further reducing comprehension. The system had the same limitations as traditional Morse code.

The Haskins research team soon realized that the limitations of its reading machine derived from a fundamental property of human speech.[4] Linguists had thought that the sounds of speech were similar to "beads on a string." Each sound supposedly was independent of its neighbors. Like the movable type used to print books, each speech sound was thought to be an independent entity that could be combined with any other letter sound, subject to some restrictions (some sound patterns could not occur in particular languages, for instance, *ng* at the start of a word in English). However, the fundamental premise was that people listened to each sound in sequence, identifying it from the acoustic "cues" in the segment of time that corresponded to the individual sound and then went on to identifying the next sound, stringing the identified segments into syllables and words. W. Freeman Twaddell, a distinguished linguist at Brown University in the 1930s and 1940s, had provided an explicit model of how people were supposed to identify the individual "phonemes," the meaningful speech sounds, and put them together into words, phrases, and sentences. One simple example will illustrate this hypothetical process. Three phonemes [c] [a] [t] make up the word *cat* (a phonemic transcription would use the symbols [c] [æ] and [t], but the alphabetic symbols will suffice). Each phoneme is hypothetically identified in sequence from acoustic "cues" that signal each sound. The key claim is that the acoustic cues for each sound are confined to a particular segment of time. Each phoneme is therefore independent of its neighbors. Three independent phonemes [s] [a] [p] hypothetically make up the word *sap*. If we isolate the phonemes that constitute *cat* and *sap*, we should be able to recombine them to produce the words *sat, cap, pat*. However, though elegant and simple, this model of speech production and perception is wrong.

The first hint that this model was wrong came from a project at Columbia University that used the then new technology of tape recording to build up a library of individual phonemes that could be pieced together to produce speech. The would-be inventors reasoned that it should be possible to have trained announcers carefully read a list of words and then cut out the segments of recording tape for each phoneme. Since phonemes were supposed to be the sound equivalents of movable type, it should have been possible to recombine them by means of a mechanical device that could rapidly play the stored tape segments in specified sequences. Using this system, one should have been able to form the word *tack* by rearranging the three phonemes that formed the word *cat*. However, when the system was constructed with the state-of-the-art technology of the 1950s, the resulting sounds were incomprehensible. One person who worked on that project described the resulting signal as the "speech of a drunken cockroach." Attempts to improve the system focused on the mechanics of the tape playback system, but the sound never improved. The inherent problem was that when a person said the word *cat*, the acoustic cues for each sound were, in fact, distributed across the entire word.

The diagram on the next page adapted from one of the Haskins Laboratories papers illustrates this time smearing. The acoustic cues are melded together. The term used to describe this process is *encoding*. The primary acoustic cue that lets you identify the first consonant of *bag*, [b æ g] in phonetic transcription, as a [b] rather than a [d] or [g] is impressed on the segment of time that also lets you know that you're hearing the vowel [æ]. (The brackets before and after a letter indicate that it refers to a sound of the International Phonetic Alphabet, a set of symbols used to transcribe the sounds of speech.) The cues for the final [t] sound are likewise distributed throughout the vowel. The vowel's acoustic cues are distributed throughout the entire monosyllabic word. Furthermore, it is inherently impossible to cut out a "pure" [b], because the acoustic cues for the vowel [æ] were impressed on the initial [b] when it was spoken. The encoding process chunks the speech signal into syllable-size segments as you talk. The human speech perception system operates in terms of these longer syllable-size chunks of speech, which obviously occur at a lower rate than the individual phonemes. The human speech perception system is complex; it is not the sort of system that an engineering group would have designed. In principle, it would have been simpler if each sound were independent.

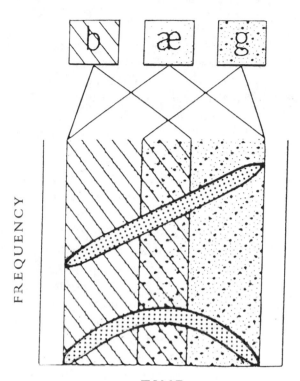

FREQUENCY

TIME

1-1—Encoded Acoustic Signal of *bag*
The acoustic cues that convey the individual sounds of speech that roughly correspond to the letters of the alphabet are melded together. Two of the formant frequencies that specify the word *bag* are represented by the shaded bars. The formant patterns that convey the sounds [b] and [g] are spread across two-thirds of the syllable impressed on the [æ] vowel. (Based on Liberman et al. 1968)

Speech Is a Five-Ring Circus

The gymnastics that humans use to produce speech are likewise complex. As we talk, we must continually plan ahead, modifying the immediate movements of our speech-producing organs—our lips, tongue, larynx, lungs, and velum (a structure that can seal the nose from the mouth)—to take account of what we're *going* to say. Another simple experiment will reveal this process.

EXPERIMENT 2

1. Stand in front of a mirror and look at your lips as you say the vowel [i] (we'll use phonetic notation henceforth), the vowel of the word *see.* Now say the word *Sue,* which has the vowel [u]. You'll see that your lips have moved forward and closed in order to produce the vowel [u]. These lip gestures, often termed "rounding" in phonetics texts, are necessary to produce the vowel [u].

2. Now say the word *tie.* If you carefully watch your face, you'll see that you don't round your lips at the start of the word. Now say *too,* which contains the vowel [u]. If your speech producing system is working correctly, you will round your lips at the start of the word when you are articulating the initial [t], anticipating the [u] that is produced "after" the initial [t]. Your speech production has been encoded. The rounding of the initial [t] of *too* makes its acoustic properties different from the "same" sound, the [t] of *tie.* Experiments in which speech has been manipulated by a computer show that listeners will hear the "entire" words *too* and *tea* on hearing about 20/1000 of a second of the two acoustically different [t]s.[5]

The exact timing between lips and the movement of the tongue tip that's necessary to produce a [t] seems to vary for different languages and dialects. Two American speech scientists, James Lubker and Tom Gay, who were working at the Royal Institute of Technology's Speech Laboratory in Stockholm, showed that native speakers of Swedish, for example, seem to anticipate rounded vowels to a greater degree than native speakers of English. The distinction probably forms part of what we normally think of as a "Swedish accent." This Swedish versus English distinction obviously isn't part of the genetic endowment of the population of Sweden. Research on the acquisition of speech by children that Joan Sereno, who is now at Cornell University, and I conducted showed that English-speaking children learn to perform these articulatory gymnastics between the ages of three and five years. They appear to be unconsciously paying attention to these subtle distinctions, which they gradually learn to mimic by a process of trial and error. The articulatory maneuvers that people use to produce speech are arguably the most complex that ordinary people attain during their lifetime.[6] Research on the acquisition of speech by normal children shows that they don't really attain adult levels of proficiency until about the age of ten years.

Why Is the Speech Perception-Production Process So Complex?

No other living species has the anatomy and the brain mechanisms that humans use to produce speech. Although chimpanzees are the closest living relatives of modern human beings, they cannot produce even simple words. Comparative analyses of human and chimpanzee DNA and the fossil evidence indicate that humans and chimpanzees had a common ancestor a mere five million years ago. Some fundamental differences exist between the sound-producing anatomy of chimpanzees and that of humans. However, despite these anatomical differences, discussed in the chapters that follow, chimpanzees would be able to produce a muffled approximation to human speech *if* their brains were capable of planning and executing the necessary complex articulatory maneuvers. But even though experimenters and animal trainers have assiduously attempted to teach chimpanzees to talk since the seventeenth century, no chimpanzee has ever been able to speak. It is becoming evident that human speech ability depends on two factors—specialized anatomy and a special-purpose neural "functional language system" that regulates speech production, speech perception, and syntax in the human brain. Both anatomy and brain had to evolve from the primate base of the human-ape common ancestor to make human speech, language, thought, and culture possible. And both appear to have reached the human condition in Eve. But why is the system so complex?

Darwin's Solution

The answer to this question derives from what Ernst Mayr, one of the great minds of twentieth-century evolutionary biology, terms the "proximate logic" of evolution. In simple terms, evolution is miserly and opportunistic. The goal is to achieve a result by spending as little as possible and making do with what you already have. The time resolution of the "standard" mammalian auditory system seems to be about the same for both primitive and evolved mammalian species. Patricia Kuhl, a psychologist at the University of Washington who studies both children and animals, for example, found that chinchillas and humans used the same temporal criteria to tell whether a sound was a [d] or a [t]. The distinction here rests on the timing between the moment the vocal cords of the larynx begin to move open and shut in a regular manner, producing "phonation," and the moment your lips open, producing a "puff" or "burst" of air noise. If the noise burst and phonation occur within 20 msec (a msec is 1/1000 of a second), both the chinchilla and the human will "hear" the sound [b]. A longer time delay yields a [p]. The decision-making criterion seems to be the length of time that must intervene between two different sounds in order for the hearer reliably to know which occurred first. Human beings and chinchillas use the same auditory criterion to categorize these sounds because humans retain the basic "primitive" mammalian auditory system found in chinchillas.[7]

Evolutionary biologists find it essential to distinguish between "primitive" and "derived" features when they chart the family trees of various species. A primitive feature is one that characterizes an ensemble of species that are the ancestors of a particular species. A derived feature is one that differentiates a species and its close relatives from other, less related species. For example, frogs, chickens, monkeys, and humans normally have five digits, a primitive feature shared by most terrestrial animals. Single hooves are a derived feature differentiating horses and closely related species from other mammals. But we couldn't conclude that human beings are more closely related to frogs than horses because we and frogs have five digits. Human beings simply retain the primitive five-finger, five-toe configuration of terrestrial animals.

We also retain most aspects of the primitive mammalian auditory system. As Experiment 1 showed, we, like chinchillas and other rodents, are unable temporally to resolve sounds that occur at rates that are much above ten sounds per second. When sounds are presented at a rate that exceeds fifteen per second, they merge into a continuous buzz. The complex human speech system is a typical case of evolutionary tinkering. We have retained the general-purpose "primitive" mammalian auditory system and simply added a special-purpose speech-encoding system that handles a specific function.

This evolutionary solution for speech is similar in some ways to the way human visual ability has been enhanced by the addition of a new system that coordinates pupil size in both eyes to an older, primitive system found in frogs and other amphibians. The primitive system adjusts the pupil opening of each eye according to the light intensity falling on that eye. If more light falls on one eye, its pupil size will contract; the pupil size of the other eye depends solely on the light falling on that eye. The system is localized and does not involve the central brain. In contrast, a second system, which has as its "design objective" contrast enhancement, has been added to the older, primitive system. If we were "logically" constructed, it would have been more "economical" simply to replace the old system. But evolution is not "logical." The "new" contrast-enhancing visual system coordinates the pupil size of both eyes through central brain regulation, overriding the older primitive system that remains in place. In consequence, one standard neurological test for damage to the brain involves shining a bright light into one eye. If the brain is intact, both eyes will have the same pupil opening. If the pupils have different openings, it's a sign that the central brain is not working normally, allowing the primitive system to take over.

In the chapters that follow I will present evidence showing that both the anatomy and the brain mechanism involved in speech production are the results of evolution "tinkering" with devices that originally were used for other purposes. Our mouth, throat, and larynx (the Adam's apple forms part of the larynx, sometimes called the voice box) were originally "designed" for swallowing food and breathing. They were modified so that we could produce sounds that were easier to understand; the evolutionary tinkering is apparent in the fact that the rearranged human combination speech-eating-breathing anatomy makes us susceptible to choking to death when food lodges in the larynx. Such tinkering also appears to have adapted brain mechanisms that may once have been designed to control precise hand gestures to regulate speech production, syntax, and thinking. And the fossil evidence indicates that these anatomical and brain systems first attained their modern state in some Eve and/or Adam who probably lived in Africa some 150,000 years ago.

CHAPTER 2

Chimpanzees and Time Machines

ROM TIME TO TIME the junk mail includes an offer to "research" the genealogy of the Liebermans and to provide a family tree and crest. Although it would be amusing to design our "ancestral" crest (a word processor crossed with an ice ax and a Neanderthal skull?), the breathlessly worded prospectus goes directly into the recycling bin. You would really need a time machine to make a family tree of our family, because the records were lost long ago, if they were ever kept. We likewise would need a time machine that would allow us to travel back five million years or so, to observe the behavior of the common ancestor of apes and humans. This poses a problem since our goal is to determine how and why we are so different from other living species. If we could see how our distant ancestors acted, as Charles Darwin put it, in their "infinitely complex relations with organic beings and external nature," we could begin to sort out the pieces of the puzzle. We could also study their brains and bodies, noting the differences between them and us, ultimately determining the meaningful physiological characteristics that underlie human language and thought.

But though time travel is fiction, we can study the past with one of the tools that Darwin invented. Darwin realized that the process of natural selection operates to adapt living organisms to particular environments—particular ecological "niches." So although mammals evolved from reptiles that have been extinct for more than 200 million years, similar reptiles survive in the ecological niches for which they are well adapted. Comparative studies of the brains and bodies of living reptiles literally flesh out the fossilized bones of the therapsids, the first mammal-like reptiles. Moreover, we can get some reasonable notion of how therapsids behaved by observing present-day reptiles. The comparative method, relating observations of living animals that are in the family tree of extinct species to their extinct cousins, can lead to surprising conclusions. When I was a boy, the Walt Disney version of the demise of the dinosaurs showed them shuffling along, too slow to escape the flowing lava and mud. Later comparative studies showed that some dinosaurs ran. (Steven Spielberg had done his homework in filming *Jurassic Park,* when he showed toothy dinosaurs racing toward their prey.)

Since it is apparent that most of the bones, brains, and bodies of living chimpanzees are homologous with those of humans—meaning that we and they share a distant common ancestor—we have a window onto that distant time. Behavior is an aspect of culture that is difficult to infer from the archaeological record of early human evolution. Chimpanzee field studies again allow us to make some reasonable inferences concerning the behavior of our earliest hominid ancestors and the baseline conditions of cognition and language at the start of human evolution.

Chimpanzee Culture

One factor that clearly sets human beings apart from other living animals is the overwhelming effect of culture on the behavior of individuals. Our genes undoubtedly affect our behavior. Jerome Kagan's research at Harvard University, for example, shows that the children of shy, introspective parents tend to be shy and introspective. However, human culture demonstrably channels the behavior of human societies and the individuals who make up those societies. The chronicles of history repeatedly show profound changes in human behavior that reflect changed cultural values. People are capable of committing the most appalling atrocities or acts of kindness in the "normal" context of their culture. As human culture changes, so does behavior. The capacity to construct and modify cultures clearly must be a consequence of our cognitive/linguistic ability. In biological terms, the brain begets culture, and the capacity to form and transmit cultural values is an indirect gauge of brainpower. What, then, is the record of culture in human evolution? Is it a unique hominid attribute?

Field studies of chimpanzees in their natural habitats unequivocally demonstrate that their behavior is modified by culture as well as by their genes. Since chimpanzees clearly derive from the common ancestor of humans and apes, we can conclude that cultural transmission of human behavior was present in our earliest, extinct hominid ancestors and that they had brains that were capable of learning and transmitting complex behavior.

Jane Goodall is deservedly the world's best-known authority on chimpanzee behavior. She really founded the field. Her observations of chimpanzees in the Gombe Reserve in the East African country of Tanzania span more than forty years. Much of her work is documented in her 1986 book, *The Chimpanzees of Gombe: Patterns of Behavior.* The title is significant because in documenting patterns of behavior, Goodall is describing chimpanzee culture. This culture is complex, and Goodall has over the years spun a web of trained observers and techniques that has yielded some startling results. Though it started as a one-woman project (Goodall with binoculars and notebook), trained Tanzanian observers now follow chimpanzees in both their routine and their unusual activities, recording events with video cameras and tape-recorded field notes. The video recordings and field notes are now being cross-indexed in digital form for analysis by means of computer techniques at the Jane Goodall Institute at the University of Southern California under the direction of Chris Boehm, one of Goodall's longtime colleagues.

Many of the attributes of human culture that were once thought to be unique are part of Gombe chimpanzee culture. Anthropology texts, for example, used to start the discussion of human evolution with the phrase "man the toolmaker," implying (*a*) that toolmaking was a unique human attribute and (*b*) that it was the key to the evolution of the human brain. The Gombe research group shattered that illusion. Some of the most compelling evidence came from chimpanzee gourmet cuisine. Termites apparently constitute a seasonal caviar-like treat. During the main termite season, October to December, the Gombe chimpanzees make and carry termite-fishing wands with them. The wands vary in length and manufacturing complexity. The chimpanzees use grasses, vines, twigs, and other smooth and pliable objects that can be inserted into the narrow, twisting passages of termite mounds. The would-be termite fisher inserts the wand into the termite mound and then rapidly pulls it out, eating the succulent termites clinging to the wand. Chimpanzee gourmets carefully select only the most suitable termite-fishing wands. The wands vary in length from seven to one hundred centimeters. At the height of the termite season chimpanzees will settle in for prolonged termite-fishing sessions at a suitable termite mound, bringing extra fishing wands along, which they keep in reserve. Ants sometimes constitute the taste thrill and are gathered by similar techniques and shorter fishing wands. Repeated observations show that, in Goodall's words,

the chimpanzee, with his advanced understanding of the relations between things, can modify objects to make them suitable for a particular purpose. And he can to some extent modify them to "a regular and set pattern." He can pick up, even prepare, an object that he will subsequently use as a tool at a location that may be quite out of sight. Most important of all, he can use an object as a tool to solve a completely novel problem. (Goodall 1986, 536)

Goodall's pioneering work led others to observe chimpanzees in different, geographically isolated parts of Africa. Their studies show, beyond any reasonable doubt, that *culture* and environment rather than genes determine the particular tools and techniques that chimpanzees use. In the Tai region of West Africa the Swiss ethologists Christian and Hedwige Boesch have filmed chimpanzees using stone and wood hammers and anvils to crack open nuts. Gombe chimpanzees do not have this particular technology, nor do the Tai chimpanzees fish with termite sticks. Like that of human beings, their technology is the product of genetically endowed cognitive and manipulative capacity shaped by time and culture. William McGrew[1] lists thirty-four different populations of chimpanzees in Africa that have been observed making and using tools. McGrew, a specialist on primate tool use, also concludes that chimpanzees have a "tool-kit":

> Chimpanzees are the only non-human species in nature to use different tools to solve different problems. They go beyond using the same tool to solve different problems (e.g. a sponge of leaves to swab out a fruit or a cranial cavity) or different tools to solve the same problem (e.g. probes *or* bark *or* grass *or* vine to fish for termites). Thus they have a *tool-kit*. (McGrew 1993, 158)

McGrew's description of an eleven-year-old female chimpanzee at work in the Gambia makes this point clear:

> She first used a stout stick chisel (with active palmer grip) to break into the outer surface of the arboreal bee's nest, then a finer-pointed chisel (with active and passive palmer grip) to widen the indentation. Then she punctured the wall of the nest with a bodkin (gripped in the teeth as well as hand!), and finally she used a dip-stick probe (with modified pencil grip) to extract the honey. (McGrew 1993, 159)

The tools that chimpanzees use are simple, but it is significant that they appear consciously to fabricate and use tools to achieve specific ends. The simplicity of chimpanzee tools is in this context irrelevant. What is important is that the chimpanzees anticipate and plan ahead for tasks that involve using a tool.

In the context of chimpanzee culture the simplicity of the tools does not tell us anything about the toolmaking limitations of the chimpanzee brain. Would human beings raised in a cultural setting in which stone tools were not used spontaneously fabricate stone tools? One chimpanzee reared in a human, tool-using culture has learned to make paleolithic stone tools. Nicholas Toth of Indiana University, an expert on stone tools, made some simple stone tools,[2] while Kanzi, a pygmy chimpanzee at the Yerkes Language Research Center near Atlanta, Georgia, observed him. Kanzi copied Toth and made his own stone tools without additional instruction. The complexity of human tools is clearly a function of the transmission of technology through the medium of *culture*. If you reflect on the matter, think about the tools that *you* could make if you were somehow plucked out of your chair and placed, naked, in a forest without even a Swiss army knife. And you would have the benefit of your knowledge of toolmaking that was the result of at least 300,000 years of human experimentation with tools and toolmaking.

It is, in fact, very difficult to make inferences concerning the cognitive abilities of our hominid ancestors from the archaeological record of stone and bone tools that have survived from past epochs. Ian Davidson, an Australian archaeologist who has an encyclopedic knowledge of the human tool record, has argued that modern human language and thinking appeared only 35,000 years ago, because that is the period in which we see some evidence for the start of an ever accelerating pace of *change* and improvements in tools and toolmaking technology. However, Davidson's linking of technological change so directly to thinking ability is unwarranted, because tool complexity clearly is a product as much of culture as of cognition. Though we now have laser-guided bombs and tanks, humans as a group are neither more nor less intelligent than the Achaeans and Trojans who fought before the walls of Troy hurling rocks and bronze-tipped spears at each other. Could a thirtieth-century archaeologist conclude that some quantum jump in human

cognitive ability occurred in the short space of 200 years by comparing the remains of Boeing 747 aircraft to George Washington's
horse-drawn coach? Can we thus conclude that the human beings
who lived 100,000 years ago and had modern-looking skulls were
stupider than somewhat more modern-appearing humans who lived
35,000 years ago and had fancier stone and bone tools?

Culture, through the medium of language, transmits human
technology. Chimpanzee technology is simple, but its presence is a
sure sign that the biological foundations for the cognitive and linguistic abilities that underlie human culture and technology were
present in our distant hominoid ancestor, the common ancestor of
present-day chimpanzees and people. Conversely, the sameness of
chimpanzee technology indicates that some *biological* distinction
that yields human cognitive-linguistic ability differentiates us from
them. In this light, the almost unchanged nature of the stone tools
used by *Homo erectus* for almost two million years perhaps reflects a
meaningful cognitive and linguistic discontinuity between modern
human beings and these extinct beings. However, when did
hominids start to make tools, and what can this tell us about
human evolution?

No reasonable person would claim that the detailed characteristics of the tools that we use are the result of an innate, genetically
transmitted neural "tool organ." Practically everyone can remember the era before the cellular phone, the Walkman, and the laptop
computer. Even casual knowledge of different cultures gleaned
from documentary films and videos reveals the variety of tool
forms used by people living in different parts of the world. Culture
and chance overwhelmingly determine whether an individual
ends up earning a living by shaping wood planks with a kukri or
words with a computer keyboard. Studies of chimpanzees living
apart in different regions of Africa likewise show that different tool
technologies are used in geographically isolated chimpanzee cultures. Moreover, these studies show that we cannot attribute these
different technologies to the chimpanzees' genes; chimpanzees are
not like spiders, which are genetically programmed to build webs.
Chimpanzees transmit toolmaking techniques as well as other

aspects of behavior from one generation to the next through the medium of culture, not their genes. The filmed records of Christian and Hedwige Boesch in the Tai region of the Ivory Coast in East Africa show chimpanzee parents teaching young chimpanzees the art of nut cracking with hammers and anvils. The adult chimpanzees probably wouldn't meet teacher–certification standards in your local elementary school, but they are pedagogues. The Boesches have repeatedly observed chimpanzee mothers and one adult male overtly tutoring young chimpanzees in the art of nut cracking. The adult tutors sometimes move the young chimpanzee's hands into position on the hammer; they sometimes align the hammer, nut, and anvil; they sometimes simply interrupt an inept pupil and demonstrate the correct technique. Pedagogy itself thus is not a unique aspect of human culture.[3] It clearly can be practiced without complex language.

Chimpanzees live together in complex groups of mothers and their adolescent and younger children, "courting" male-female pairs that go off to be together, gangs of males, and various combinations of the individual chimpanzees that make up the group. The "alpha," or dominant, males who usually are at the top of chimpanzee society attain their rank, as often as not, by what would in humans pass for statesmanship and cunning. The alpha male does not keep his place by necessarily being stronger and fiercer than other chimpanzees. Chimpanzees seem to be constantly networking; alliances often count for more than physical strength. Cleverness and cunning are typically qualities for survival; wily Ulysses returned home from the siege of Troy.

The field observations of chimpanzees living in the state of nature show that cunning is not an exclusively human attribute. The lame chimpanzee Figan, for example, became the dominant male of the Gombe group by terrorizing the competition by banging on an empty metal oil can. Figan literally drummed his way to the top of the group. Furthermore, it is clear that an established social hierarchy exists in chimpanzee society. For chimpanzees, as for human beings, it helps to be the son or daughter of "high born" parents. Richard Wrangham in his Tanzanian field observations has found that being the offspring of a high-ranked female is a necessary condition for a male chimpanzee's success in that chimpanzee culture.

Chimpanzee mothers and their sons and daughters form tight groups and sometimes develop their own "customs," some of which are gruesome. Adult chimpanzees, for example, occasionally kill and eat infant chimpanzees. When chimpanzee cannibalism was first observed by Jane Goodall, it was in one mother-daughter "family" group and was thought to reflect an organic disease, a chimpanzee madness. One mother and her adolescent daughter were secretly killing and eating infant chimpanzees of other mothers. This activity, though unacceptable in present-day human society, would nonetheless be consistent with sociobiological theories that attempt to account for all behavior in terms of what Darwin termed "the struggle for survival." To Darwin that meant actions that would ensure that your own progeny would survive and multiply, so killing and eating the infants of other chimpanzees would not harm and might help improve your "biological fitness" (the current shorthand for having more surviving offspring). But chimpanzee cannibalism does not make sense in these terms either, since male chimpanzees have been observed killing and eating their *own* infants. Pervasive cannibalism of this type, therefore, cannot be explained by sociobiological theories. Nor can the absence of cannibalism be explained by them; it must stem from a moral code. Cannibalism appears to have been part of accepted "normal" human behavior in many past societies, so chimpanzees are not exceptional in this respect. The development of a human moral code is, in fact, an issue that I'll return to in Chapter 6.

Chimpanzees in general are not very peaceable creatures in the state of nature. They supplement their vegetable, termite, and ant diet with meat and systematically hunt monkeys and other smaller animals, using tactics that do not differ substantially from those used by nineteenth-century English gentry on their country estates. Pheasants were driven toward the waiting shooters by lines of beaters. In the Tai, chimpanzees drive terrified monkeys through the trees into the clutches of other chimpanzees lying in ambush.

So we again can't claim that hunting was the key for the evolution of human language and thinking. The "man the hunter" theory doesn't supply either a defining quality of human nature or the hypothetical activity that set the stage for the evolution of human beings. The search never seems to end for the discovery of some supposedly unique aspect of human culture that, in itself, would have triggered the evolution of human language and thinking. According to one recent script, the primary function of human language is gossip, by which we supposedly maintain "group identity." (My Jewish mother would have called this the "yenta" theory of language.) Idle chatter, according to this theory, allows large groups of people to maintain group cohesiveness. Taciturn Swedes, beware—you will be extinguished.

Chimpanzee Warfare

Although virtually all human civilizations deplore casual violence, we celebrate the heroic feats of Achilles and Hector and David's slaying of Goliath, and long-forgotten civilizations celebrated battles and wars lost in time. Warfare seems to be a human "universal." Some other group becomes the enemy, and violent deeds that would otherwise be punished are celebrated. But how to define the enemy? In George Orwell's anti-utopian novel *1984,* the Ministry of Truth, through the medium of language, continually identified the ever-changing enemy; East-Asia was the enemy and West-Asia our ally, now West-Asia is the enemy, and so on. In the short span of fifty years the enemies and allies of the United States of America have shifted. Unlike sheep, human societies no longer have "natural" enemies other than invisible microorganisms. We use the medium of language to identify the enemy state or group. Again we can look at the Gombe chimpanzee history to find this human pattern of warfare, and its linguistic implications probably were present in our distant common hominoid ancestor.

In 1972 Jane Goodall and her research team realized that the

Gombe chimpanzee group they had been studying had split in two. The area in which the Gombe chimpanzees lived had gradually been divided into two north-south territories populated by chimpanzees that had previously "frequently encountered each other without undue hostility" (Goodall 1986, 503). The northern subgroup contained eight fully mature males; the southern Kahama group, six. Goodall's account of the "war" and annihilation of the Kahama group (pp. 503–34) documents the encounters of raiding parties patrolling the borders of the disputed territories and attacks to kill. Although the chimpanzees' raiding parties didn't have the tactical skills of the Roman legions, their behavior was that of warriors engaged in battle, "with the ability to use weapons for hurting or killing . . . [free] from the inhibitions and social sanctions that operate within the group . . . [committing] acts that would not be tolerated within the group" (p. 532). The chimpanzees of the Kahama, having previously "enjoyed close and friendly relations with their aggressors," were systematically hunted down and exterminated. The level of cognitive and linguistic ability that is necessary to transform friends into foes is clearly present in living chimpanzees and undoubtedly was present in the common ancestor of apes and humans. It is also clear that the high level of human cognitive-linguistic ability is not necessary to transmit these "geopolitical" distinctions.

Chimpanzee Language

Field studies of chimpanzees show that they act like humans in many other ways. Ritualized "courtship" and changing alliances aimed at achieving dominant status within the group are common. And regional, culturally determined differences have been observed in the geographically isolated groups of chimpanzees studied over the past thirty years. However, no chimpanzee has ever talked or even attempted to mimic human speech. Field observations indeed suggest that chimpanzee vocalizations are "bound" entities triggered by the chimpanzee's emotional state.

Jane Goodall, who arguably has heard more chimpanzee communications than any other person, notes,

> Chimpanzee vocalizations are closely bound to emotion. The production of a sound in the *absence* of the appropriate emotional state seems to be an almost impossible task for a chimpanzee. . . .
>
> Chimpanzees can learn to *suppress* calls in situations when the production of sounds might, by drawing attention to the signaler, place him in an unpleasant or dangerous situation, but even this is not easy. On one occasion when Figan was an adolescent, he waited in camp until the senior males had left and we were able to give him some bananas (he had had none before). His excited food calls quickly brought the big males racing back and Figan lost his fruit. A few days later he waited behind again, and once more received his bananas. He made no loud sounds, but the calls could be heard deep in his throat, almost causing him to gag. (Goodall 1986, 125)

Although psychologists and linguists still dispute how human children learn to talk, everyone agrees that a normal child reared in any human culture will usually start to talk before the third year of life. By the age of five virtually all children talk at length. Conversely, we know that children raised in the absence of exposure to language in the early years of life never develop normal linguistic or normal cognitive ability. In contrast, individuals suffering severe forms of mental retardation like Down's syndrome never acquire normal language even when they are raised by loving parents.[4] Exposure to some normal human child-rearing environment, therefore, appears to be a necessary and sufficient condition for the acquisition of language by children, *if* they have the necessary neural equipment that is normally present in human beings. This being the case, we can explore the full linguistic potential of the chimpanzee brain by rearing chimpanzees in a human environment.

A cross-fostering chimpanzee experiment involves raising a chimpanzee as though it were a human child, exposing it to both "normal" human conversation and to the "motherese" variety of speech commonly directed toward young children. Keith and Cathy Hayes did this in the 1950s. They raised the infant chimpanzee Viki together with their son. At the start of the project Viki was "completely unable to make any sound at all on purpose." But the Hayeses persisted and added intensive speech training (for instance, they manipulated Viki's lower jaw), which no one would ever apply in any normal human context, to Viki's daily routines. Viki in many ways began to act like a human child. However, when the project ended because of her premature death from encephalitis when she was barely seven years old, she could produce only four human words, which were scarcely intelligible. At about the time that it was becoming apparent that apes lacked the anatomy and neural control necessary to produce human speech, a different approach to the cross-fostering experiment was started by Beatrix and Alan Gardner. The Gardners' academic training would at first seem to have made them unlikely chimpanzee "parents." Alan Gardner was a psychologist studying rats. Beatrix had just completed a thesis on the three-spined stickleback fish. The immediate stimulus for their cross-fostering chimpanzee project was the demonstration that early environment drastically affects the mental and social development of primates. Harry Harlow, a distinguished psychologist, had shown the dramatic effects of childhood neglect on monkeys. The monkey infants clung tenaciously to stuffed surrogate monkey mother figures, but monkey infants raised without their mothers became asocial and "retarded." The monkeys' early deprived social environment clearly affected their development. The Gardners proposed to see what would happen if a chimpanzee was raised as though it were human in a linguistic environment that involved not speech but American Sign Language (ASL). Would the early rich human linguistic environment bring out whatever linguistic potential existed in the chimpanzee?

ASL is not a manual version of English. English syntax relies to a great degree on word order to convey differences in meaning. In contrast, ASL uses locations in space to convey distinctions in meaning. Particular hand formations, roughly equivalent to the nouns and verbs of English, are produced in a particular "signing space," an area in which the sign may be made. Distinctions conveyed by serial order in English, such as the subject and object, are conveyed by moving the sign gesture from one location to another.

The Gardners' project began in 1966 when they, in effect, became the foster parents of Washoe, a ten-month-old female chimpanzee captured in Africa and named for the county of Nevada in which she lived with the Gardners and their research team until 1970. During that period she was treated like a child, albeit one in contact with an adult during all of her waking hours. Washoe from the start was diapered, clothed, and given shoes. As she matured, she learned to use cups and spoons and to help clear the table after dinner. She learned to use the toilet, played with toys, broke some, and, like young children, observed language in its ordinary uses. Washoe, in other words, observed ASL conversations between adults and communications in ASL directed toward her, although the adults did not necessarily expect her to understand what was being signed in the early stages of the project.

Aside from a few practice sessions analogous to those in which many parents attempt to "teach" young children how to pronounce words more distinctly, Washoe learned ASL words as might a human child raised in the same environment. The scientific world was startled to learn that Washoe "acquired" about fifty ASL words in the first year of cross-fostering. Words are powerful conceptual as well as communicative elements. When we think of the word *tree,* it doesn't necessarily refer to a particular tree or even a species of trees. *Tree*, furthermore, codes a fuzzy concept. How do we differentiate between a bush and a tree?

Linguists rightly consider words to be one of the defining characteristics of human language. Prior to Washoe's feat, words *were* supposed to be the defining characteristic of human language. Even Noam Chomsky, whose focus has been the syntax of human language, considered the ability to use words the key to human language. Norman Geschwind, one of the most productive neurologists of the twentieth century, went so far as to "prove" that the brains of apes precluded their acquiring words. (The ape brain supposedly lacked hypothetical cortical "association" areas.)

The firestorm that broke when the Gardners published their first paper on ape language, in 1969, in the prestigious journal *Science*, has not subsided. Objections were raised immediately. Some scholars simply wanted to see more data published. Others claimed that Washoe was merely "parroting" a set of memorized hand gestures to obtain rewards, a sort of super-rat trained by the methods favored by psychologists in the 1960s. One can train rats, for example, to perform a series of acrobatic feats—jumping through hoops, tumbling, jumping up, etc.—by patiently rewarding them with food for one "trick" and then linking that trick to another one.

Other objections were bizarre. The linguist Thomas Sebeok organized a conference in 1986 whose aim was to show that all ape-language experiments were contaminated by the "Clever Hans" phenomenon. The phenomenon refers to a famous experiment that seemed to show that a horse named Hans was able to count numbers. This happened long ago, when the kaiser still ruled Germany. Hans's trainer, Wilhelm von Osten, honestly believed that Hans could count. Osten would call out two numbers. Hans would then tap his hoof until he reached the correct sum. Hans was the toast of Berlin until 1907, when it was realized that though Hans was truly a clever horse, he couldn't count. Hans had learned through observation to associate minute changes in Osten's facial expression with getting a carrot by stamping his foot. Osten unknowingly tensed his facial muscles when Hans's hoof taps approached the correct sum.

Inadvertent "cueing" effects still plague psychological and linguistic research. Many of the "facts" cited by linguists to support the claim that children effortlessly learn arcane facts about human language are artifacts of flawed experiments in which children have learned to respond to cues unwittingly provided by the adult investigators. However, the Gardners were quite aware of Clever Hans and went to great lengths to avoid similar errors. Washoe and the other four chimpanzee infants whom the Gardners raised in cross-fostered "families" in the continuation of this project gradually acquired and productively used about 140 different ASL signs over the sixty-month span of Project Washoe. The elaborate procedures that the Gardners used to test the vocabularies of the chimpanzees absolutely ruled out the Clever Hans effect.

Even a short account of the basic design and procedures of Project Washoe will demonstrate that chimpanzees have brains that allow them to acquire some aspects of human language, albeit in reduced form. Starting in November 1972 four newborn chimpanzees were placed in four adoptive families at the Gardners' ranch laboratory in the suburbs of Reno, Nevada. The four chimpanzees, Moja, Pili, Tatu, and Dar, were all born in American laboratories, and each arrived in Reno within a few days of birth. Each chimpanzee had a family: one or more of whose human members remained with each chimpanzee between seven in the morning and eight in the evening throughout the year. The family members were trained observers. Each family included one or more persons proficient in ASL—deaf students working toward graduate degrees in psychology, hearing persons who had deaf parents or siblings and were bilingual users of ASL, and teachers of deaf children. The family groups were stable throughout the project. Stringent criteria were adopted to determine when an ASL sign entered each chimpanzee's vocabulary. The Gardners reported,

> After three separate and independent reports of well-formed, unprompted, and appropriate observations of a sign by three different observers, we placed the new sign on the list of candidates for reliability. A sign remained on this list until there was at least one report of a well-formed, unprompted, and appropriate observation on each of fifteen consecutive days. We restarted the count after any day without a qualified report. After meeting the fifteen day criterion, the sign was added to the list of reliable vocabulary items. The record of the fifteen day criteria period contained independent reports by most if not all of the members of the foster family. . . . Each report also had to be judged as spontaneous and appropriate by at least three familiar human companions. It was spontaneous if it

appeared without informative prompting—such as direct modelling or guidance that could have induced any portion of the target sign [such as a hand shape or placement on the face of one of the human family members signing to each other or the chimpanzee]. It was appropriate if it suited the verbal and situational context. The staff decided, for example, that SODAPOP was inappropriate for juice and CANDY was inappropriate for gum. (Gardner and Gardner 1971, 140–41)

The cross-fostered chimpanzees' ASL vocabularies were also formally tested. The vocabulary test for chimpanzees was a model of experimental correctness. Each chimpanzee sat alone in a chamber looking out at a screen on which color slides of various objects *that the chimpanzee had never seen before* were projected. The chimpanzee's task was to name each object. Since young chimpanzees' ASL signing, like young children's speech, is imperfect, it was necessary to rule out observers' "seeing" more than the chimpanzees were producing. Therefore, two observers who could not see the projected images or each other both recorded each chimpanzee's ASL signs. The two observers' transcriptions of the chimpanzees' ASL signs for 760 trials agreed 90 percent of the time. The consistency of these transcriptions compares closely to that of trained phoneticians transcribing tape recordings of the speech of young children whose pronunciation is also imperfect.

It was noted time and again by the Gardners and disinterested observers such as William Stokoe, a leading expert on ASL, that the cross-fostered chimpanzees used ASL productively and spontaneously. The Gardners' succinct description, which fits my own observations of the cross-fostered chimpanzees signing some ten years after the end of Project Washoe, is correct and convincing. Their comments, written years after Project Washoe was abruptly terminated, capture their warm feelings toward their chimpanzee foster beings:

Washoe, Moja, Pili, Tatu, and Dar signed to friends and to strangers. They signed to themselves and to each other, to dogs, cats, toys, tools, even to trees. We did not have to tempt them with treats or ply them with questions to get them to sign to us. Most of the signing was initiated by the young chimpanzees rather than by the human adults. They commonly named objects and pictures of objects in situations in which we were unlikely to reward them.

When Washoe signed to herself in play, she was usually in a private place—high in a tree or alone in her bedroom before going to sleep. All of the cross-fosterlings signed to themselves when leafing through magazines and picture books, but Washoe resented our attempts to join in this activity. If we persisted in joining her or if we watched her too closely, she often abandoned the magazine or picked it up and moved away. On one occasion, she indicated a certain advertisement, signed THAT FOOD, then looked at her hand closely and changed the phrase to THAT DRINK, which was correct. (Gardner and Gardner, in press)

A single paper that misrepresented the Gardners' work ended Project Washoe. Herbert Terrace and his colleagues at Columbia University also succeeded in publishing a paper in *Science*. Terrace's group had failed to teach a young chimpanzee to use ASL productively. Its procedure, however, was quite unlike the Gardners'. Instead of placing his chimpanzee, named Nim after the linguist Noam Chomsky, in a nurturing, stimulating, humanlike environment, Terrace relentlessly drilled him in a sterile, prisonlike environment. From the age of nine months Nim was put in an empty eight-by-eight-foot room, painted a uniform white except for a one-way mirror set into one wall. There an ever-changing staff of "teachers," who were themselves novices in ASL, attempted to teach the chimpanzee ASL. As Terrace himself noted, the would-be teachers "cycled through Project Nim in a revolving door manner." Nim failed to acquire ASL; he didn't converse. Nim had learned to repeat signs. That wasn't surprising, since any normal human child probably would have failed to acquire language and have been rendered psychotic in an equivalent situation. In fact,

Noam Chomsky had years before demonstrated that human language could not be acquired by means of the Skinnerian "operant conditioning" methods that Terrace employed.

What was surprising was the almost universal acceptance by linguists and psychologists of Terrace's conclusions. According to Terrace, the Gardners' cross-fostered chimpanzees simply "parroted," copied without comprehending, the ASL signs directed to them by their human companions. Even casual observation of documentary television films of the Gardner chimpanzees conversing in ASL revealed the hollowness of Terrace's claims. In fact, you did not have to know anything about the cross-fostered chimpanzees to recognize how absurd Terrace's claims were. Terrace held, for example, that children never repeated words, whereas the transcripts of chimpanzee conversations were full of repetitions. Any observant parent would have known that young children often repeat words. I once observed a three-year-old boy repeat the word *fan* eleven times as he sat on his father's shoulders looking at the ceiling fan above him.

However, Terrace saved the day for human uniqueness, and the upstart Gardners working in Nevada rather than at Harvard, Berkeley, or Yale were put in their place. Legions of academic psychologists had been sitting at home watching televised documentaries of Washoe signing and reading popular accounts of the Gardners' work in the *New York Times* and elsewhere. With Terrace's work the Gardners' findings seemed to have been debunked. Their research funds were cut off.

Criticism of the Gardners' work continues to the present. Entire books have been written with the express aim of debunking Project Washoe. Syntax has now become the key to human language since the cross-fostered chimpanzees, by any reasonable standard, acquired words. One book written by one of Terrace's students went so far as to assert that young human children, whose language resembles ASL chimpanzee language, do not really have any language abilities until they master syntax.

Project Washoe, didn't come to a complete halt when the funding for the elaborate and expensive cross-fostering was cut off. The cross-fostered chimpanzees were moved to Central Washington University, in Ellensburg, Washington, where Roger Fouts and his wife, Debbie, managed to keep them fed and housed. For a few years money was so short that the chimpanzees lived on day-old produce contributed by local supermarkets. However, the chimpanzees continued to sign to each other, to the new research team, and to visiting humans. When my wife, Marcia, and I visited in 1986, Washoe, Moja, Tatu, and Dar, the four surviving cross-fostered chimpanzees, signed to us as well as to the young chimpanzee Loulis, who had been raised by Washoe from infancy in an environment in which he observed only *chimpanzees* using ASL to communicate with each other and to him. Loulis was by now an indulged chimpanzee "brat" whose idea of fun was spitting at visitors. The Fouts research group virtually ceased to sign to the young adult chimpanzees and never signed when Loulis was present. Loulis nonetheless acquired ASL signs from the other signing chimpanzees.

The Limits of Chimpanzee Sign Language Ability

In the first two years of Project Washoe, the cross-fostered chimpanzees' ASL vocabularies reached 50 signs, a performance roughly equivalent to that of either hearing human children or deaf children raised from birth on in homes using ASL. Their cognitive development, evaluated by means of standard procedures, was also roughly equivalent to that of human children throughout this period. However, the performance of the chimpanzees and that of human children diverge after the age of two. When Project Washoe ended, the chimpanzees had a vocabulary of about 140 words, after sixty months of cross-fostered life. The rate, about 3 signs per month, at which they had acquired words was about the same over the entire period. This pattern stands in marked contrast to that for normal children raised under normal conditions. Near the age of three, it generally becomes very difficult to keep track of the number of words that a child knows. A "naming explosion" occurs.

Although the stringent criteria that the Gardners employed to keep track of the cross-fostered chimpanzees' vocabularies may have underestimated the extent of their true ASL vocabularies, the very fact that the same procedure could be used over the chimpanzees' first five years of life reveals a fundamental difference between chimpanzees and humans.

The chimpanzees also differed from humans with respect to their syntactic abilities. Linguists have rightly stressed the "creative" aspect of human language. Using a large, but ultimately finite, number of words, we can create an infinite number of novel sentences conveying distinctions of meaning by means of syntax. Different languages employ different methods and "rules." Chinese and English speakers can convey distinctions in meaning by means of word order. "Mary kissed John" does not carry the same message as "John kissed Mary." Other languages convey a similar actor–acted on (subject–object) distinction by inflecting or modifying words, rather than by changing their sequence. As we noted before, ASL signers move their hands to convey the object of a verb. A careful analysis of Project Washoe's ASL productions shows that two-sign phrases began to occur after the age of two and increased in number up to the age of five. Large individual differences were apparent. The chimpanzee Tatu consistently produced at least 50 percent more two-sign phrases than Moja. Tatu's phrases also were more productive than Moja's, conveying a wider range of semantic information. Three-word phrases also occurred. Typical chimpanzee ASL phrases include Dar's signing ICECREAM HURRY GIMME in response to the question WANT ICE-CREAM. The cross-fostered chimpanzees also inflected their ASL signs, though in a manner more typical of the performance of human children than that of adults. For example, the ASL sign QUIET is signed with the index finger of the signer near the signer's lips and is then moved outward toward the addressee. The chimpanzees, like young deaf children, instead placed the sign QUIET on the addressee's lips.

However, here again a quantitative difference that in reality amounts to a qualitative distinction exists between the cross-fostered chimpanzees and young children. By the age of three many children are talking their parents' ears off. If we compare the cross-fostered chimpanzees' performance with that of a bright two-year-old boy nicknamed Duff, whose tape-recorded utterances were carefully studied by Karen Landahl for her Ph.D. dissertation at Brown University, the distinction is evident. Describing a surprising episode at grandmother's house, Duff said, "woof, woof and dog wakes up and dog says woof woof and he and he up and somebody hears him calling out that window and it was mummy" (Landahl 1982, 609). The cross-fostered chimpanzees' performance at the age of five is different. They're producing about three times as many semantically different patterns as they did at age two, but the absolute number 90 is still one that can be tabulated, whereas the productive abilities of virtually any normal five-year-old child cannot. We don't know the absolute limits of chimpanzees' ASL linguistic ability, because Project Washoe was terminated when the cross-fostered chimpanzees reached the age of five. However, Project Washoe has been replicated by Duane Rumbaugh and Sue Savage-Rumbaugh, who devised a different way of communicating with chimpanzees. In short, their studies show that chimpanzees don't seem to progress beyond the language abilities of most two-and-a-half-year-old children.

Duane Rumbaugh and Sue Savage-Rumbaugh—who, like the Gardners, form a husband-wife team—have in their recent studies made use of a somewhat modified cross-fostered scheme in their ongoing ape-language studies at the Yerkes Language Research Center. Perhaps in reaction to the Gardners' muted responses to Terrace and subsequent critics, Rumbaugh and Savage-Rumbaugh are master publicists. In particular, the linguistic accomplishments of Kanzi, a bonobo, or pygmy chimpanzee, have been hailed in their research papers and films and in popular news accounts. Pygmy chimpanzees (*Pan paniscus*) form a geographically isolated subspecies of chimpanzees (*Pan troglodytes*), and Kanzi's achievements have been represented as milestones in chimpanzee language ability that reflect the superior abilities of bonobos. However, the evidence published to date (Savage-Rumbaugh and Rumbaugh 1993) indicates that

Kanzi's abilities, though superior to the other "common" chimpanzees at the Yerkes laboratories, are on a par with those of Tatu, the most proficient of the Project Washoe "common" chimpanzees.

Kanzi, like the Project Washoe chimpanzees, uses toys, goes on excursions with his human family members, is engaged in conversations directed to him, and can hear people talking to each other. In contrast to those in Project Washoe, Kanzi's human companions talk to each other and to him in English. As Nicholas Toth showed, Kanzi also learned to make simple stone tools. Kanzi's own responses are constrained to his pointing to "lexigrams" on boards or computer terminals. Each lexigram represents an English word and can, when Kanzi is using a terminal connected to a speech synthesizer, trigger the English word that corresponds to the lexigram. Using somewhat different methods, the Yerkes research group replicated the Project Washoe findings on the referential nature of Kanzi's vocabulary. The lexigrams represent concepts that correspond to the words that form the vocabularies of young human children. Kanzi also understands at least some aspects of spoken English. This finding in itself is not novel; the surviving Project Washoe chimpanzees living in Ellensburg also clearly understand at least some English words. So do most pet dogs. In our home we have to spell out words like *walk* or *going out* that would otherwise send our briard sheepdog racing to the front door attentively awaiting an excursion. We also have to spell out *cookie*. Fortunately, he has not yet learned to spell. But the formal tests of Kanzi's comprehension of English show that he surpasses that of any dog yet tested. His comprehension of English sentences was about the same as that of the two-year-old child of his human foster mother. The test material indicates that both the child and the chimpanzee can make appropriate responses to sentences that tell them to put an object into a container or to fetch something from a container or location—for example, "Go to the refrigerator to get the melon." However, this doesn't mean that either the chimpanzee or the child is using the syntactic structure of English. They simply have to know the meanings of some of the individual words of the sentence. Only one course of action is possible if they know the meanings of the words *go* or *get* and *melon* and *refrigerator*. This seems to be the case, since other test data show that Kanzi does not understand the meanings of English prepositions. Kanzi did go to the microwave oven in the laboratory and took a tomato out of it on hearing the two sentences: "Go to the microwave and get the tomato" and "Go get the tomato that's in the microwave." However, microwave ovens cannot come out of tomatoes; the chimpanzee's real-world, "semantic" knowledge is sufficient to guide his action. The array of test sentences doesn't really test any knowledge of syntax, except for one subpart in which the six-year-old chimpanzee's responses indicated that he had mastered the canonical form of English in which the subject comes before the object. Kanzi responded correctly about 75 percent of the time when he heard sentences like these: "Put the pine needles on the ball" and "Put the ball on the pine needles."

Other test data that the Yerkes group has interpreted as evidence for Kanzi's understanding complex English syntax are consistent with his having a limited attention span. (Kanzi may simply forget the beginnings of certain long sentences.) The situation is murky since in an as yet unpublished analysis of the same data, the Yerkes research group concludes that Kanzi cannot comprehend distinctions in meaning in spoken English conveyed solely by the word order.[5] Kanzi's reported lexigram combinations do not appear to make consistent use of word order to convey distinctions in meaning. In many respects they resemble the ASL communications of the Project Washoe chimpanzees. In short, Kanzi at six years seems to have about the same linguistic ability as the five-year-old Project Washoe chimpanzees.

This does not, of course, diminish the significance of the Yerkes data, which constitute a careful and independent replication of the major findings of Project Washoe. Chimpanzees clearly can acquire a 150-word vocabulary; they can combine words and infer the distinctions in meaning conveyed by the usual, primary syntactic device of the language they are exposed to (the inflectional movement pattern of ASL and the canonical subject-object word order of English). They coin new words and generally communicate at about the level of two-and-a-half-year-old children. It will be interesting to see if Kanzi and the other Yerkes chimpanzees progress beyond this level—attaining the exponential increase of vocabulary size and the mastery of syntax of human children. Other cross-fostering ape-language projects have been attempted. Lynn Myles of the University of Tennessee worked with very limited funds to cross-foster a male orangutan; the project came to an end when the ape became assertive and unmanageable. Penny Patterson, with funding from the *National Geographic Society,* worked with a gorilla. However, the absence of rigorous data recording and formal test data makes it impossible to assess the results of her project.

Chimpanzee Speech Anatomy

At about the time when the Gardners decided that it was futile to attempt to get chimpanzees to talk, I was tape-recording monkeys, chimpanzees, and gorillas in New York's Prospect and Central Park zoos. I had previously been working on the role of intonation, the "melody" of speech. Common wisdom equates speech with the larynx, sometimes called the voice box, which is located at the end of the trachea, or windpipe, which leads up from your lungs. The Adam's apple, often prominent in adult males, is the outward bulge of the thyroid cartilage, one of the cartilages that form the larynx. The larynx is a complex structure that originally evolved to protect the lungs of lungfish when they swam underwater. Monkeys, apes, and humans have similar larynges, and I had been studying texts that showed their comparative sound-producing anatomy. It was becoming apparent that apes could not talk, and I believed that I had discovered an anatomical limit on their ability to produce human speech.

Human speech is produced by a process similar to the way in which a musician playing a woodwind instrument, such as a clarinet, produces music. All woodwind instruments have a mouthpiece that contains a reed. When the player blows air through the reed, it vibrates, moving inward and outward, thereby rapidly opening and closing the air passage through the mouthpiece. Consequently air flows out of the mouthpiece of the clarinet in a series of puffs. (You would obtain a similar result if you could continually and rapidly open and close the water valve of your kitchen sink; a series of bursts of water would issue from the tap.) If you were to pull the mouthpiece out of the clarinet and listen to the air coming out of it, it would sound like a raspy, buzzing noise. The body of the clarinet, the tube that the puffs of air generated by the reed pass through, yields the musical quality of the clarinet. The notes produced by the clarinet result from the musician's changing the length of the tube that forms the clarinet's body. The clarinet's tube length determines the musical note. The physical basis of the musical note is the frequency at which the acoustic energy generated by the reed passes through the clarinet. The upper tube of the clarinet acts as a filter; that is, it lets maximum acoustic energy through at particular frequencies that correspond to the tube's length. Higher frequencies pass through shorter tubes and lower frequencies through longer tubes. Physicists and instrument makers have known this for centuries. The long pipes of a pipe organ pass maximal acoustic energy through at low frequencies; the shorter ones, at high frequencies.

When we talk, we generate a "source" of acoustic energy as the vocal cords of the larynx move inward and outward, interrupting the flow of air through the larynx. The larynx is more adaptable than the reed of a clarinet. By adjusting the muscles of the larynx, we can change the rate at which our vocal cords open and close. We perceive changes in the rate at which the periodic puffs of air issue from the larynx as the *pitch* of a person's voice. A high pitch corresponds to a rapid periodic rate, which speech scientists term the *fundamental frequency* of phonation. *Phonation* is the term used to describe the process by which the larynx produces a periodic series of puffs of air. In most human languages—for example, Chinese—changes in the pattern of fundamental frequency are used to differentiate different words. In Mandarin Chinese a level pitch for the sounds [ma] signifies *mother*. A rising pitch on [ma] signifies *hemp*.

English also uses pitch changes to signal linguistic information. At the end of a declarative sentence the pitch abruptly falls. In contrast, pitch doesn't fall at the end of a yes–no question. Pitch changes in humans, as in other animals, also signal emotion.

The major factor that differentiates words in all human languages, however, is *not* the pitch of a person's voice. The tube above the larynx, called the *supralaryngeal vocal tract* (SVT), like the clarinet's tube, filters the sound produced by the larynx. The main section of the SVT is formed by the passageway between your tongue and the back and roof of the mouth, capped by your lips. A secondary side passage through your nose can be opened by the *velum*, or soft palate, a flap of muscle and soft tissue that can be moved to seal or open your nose to the rest of the SVT. As we move our tongue, lips, larynx, and velum, we change the shape and length of the SVT. These continual changes in the shape and length of the SVT alter its filtering characteristics. The frequencies at which maximum acoustic energy would pass through the SVT therefore continually change as we talk. Speech scientists use the term *formant frequency* to describe the frequency at which maximum acoustic energy will pass through the SVT. The surprising thing about speech perception is that what we "hear" as we change our malleable SVT are the consonants and vowels of speech. In other words, what we are actually responding to when we hear the vowel [i] in the word *bee* is a particular combination of formant frequencies that differs from the combination that conveys the vowel [u] in the word *boo*.

Between the years 1967 and 1972, my colleagues Edmund Crelin, Dennis Klatt, and William Wilson and I found that human beings were the only animals on earth who had SVTs that could produce all of the sounds of human speech. The details will have to wait for the next chapter; the gist of the story is that apes, dogs, monkeys, and other animals have mouths and tongues that allow them to swallow food without the risk that it will block their larynx. Their long, relatively thin tongues are positioned almost entirely in their mouths. Their larynges are located close to the opening that leads to their nose and move upward, locking into the nose when they drink or eat. This arrangement allows them to breathe while they drink and swallow soft food. Food and drink can then pass *around* the larynx, which forms a sort of pipe placed in the middle of the food-drink pathway. In contrast, the human tongue has a round, thick cross-section. About half of your tongue is positioned in your throat, and the opening of the larynx at the base of the tongue is low. This makes human beings susceptible to choking to death when food gets caught in the larynx. It also has other negative effects, discussed in the chapters that follow, but on the positive side our anatomy allows us to make sounds like [i] and [u], which make human speech more efficient.[6]

This anatomical difference does not mean that apes could not produce an approximation to human speech. They could produce indistinct, nasalized speech if their brain were capable of controlling the muscular maneuvers that underlie speech. But they cannot. Apes therefore lack both the anatomy and the brain necessary for human speech.

Our Distant Hominid Ancestor

The chimpanzee "time machine" shows that the distant common ancestors of humans and chimpanzees had the biological capacities that underlie many of our "human" attributes. They undoubtedly made and used tools, hunted, kept track of and communicated shifting alliances, and warred among themselves. Their linguistic and cognitive abilities undoubtedly were at least as advanced as those potentially available to present-day chimpanzees. What distinguished them from chimpanzees must have been the ability to *invent* linguistic forms. As the research on the human brain's bases for thinking, syntax, and speech will show, the fact that no chimpanzee or other ape can talk may be one of the keys to understanding why our ancestors started down the path toward being human.

CHAPTER 3

He's a Big Baby

ALTHOUGH MOST ADVANCES in basic research are the results of projects specifically directed toward "advancing human understanding," that is not always true. At the end of the Second World War, the philanthropist Caryl Haskins founded a set of laboratories that he hoped would provide solutions to some real-life problems. At the time, the federal agencies that provided most of the money for the American scientific renaissance that followed were just starting to function. Haskins leased space in a run-down factory loft on Forty-third Street in New York City, close to slaughterhouses and stockyards that were being razed for the buildings that would be the home of the United Nations. The lease was his only mistake; he should have bought the building. When the lease ran out, Haskins Laboratories was forced to seek a new location, which led to my meeting Ed Crelin and the Great Neanderthal Speech War.

I was teaching at the University of Connecticut, located in rural eastern Connecticut. The university was in transition from an agricultural college. A few academic departments had brought in first-rate research teams, but it was clear from the outset that my research would take place at Haskins Laboratories, where I had a joint appointment; I had been recruited by Alvin M. Liberman, one of the moving spirits at Haskins. On Wednesday at 2 P.M. I would drive from Storrs to New Haven, park there, and then take the New Haven Railroad to New York City, returning Thursday or Friday evening (Haskins had even rented an apartment for overnight stays). New York was a perfect place for recording all sorts of primates, since it had three zoos and I was able to start work on the analysis of ape and monkey calls. However, as the new glass-walled office buildings rose around the old factory loft that housed Haskins Laboratories, so did the rent. Haskins Laboratories moved to New Haven, where a loose affiliation with Yale University was negotiated.

Though New Haven was not New York, the trip from Storrs was shorter. I also renewed contact with Arend Bouhuys, one of the world's leading experts on breathing. Arend was the sort of rosy-cheeked Dutchman you can see in Brueghel's paintings. He had guided me through the mysteries of respiratory physiology in my thesis research at MIT. Arend, Jere Mead, and Donald Procter were collaborating at the Harvard School of Public Health, studying the complex muscular adjustments that control lung activity in singing and talking. Arend would come up from Yale and Procter from Johns Hopkins University, in Baltimore. I was working along similar lines. I knew something about electronics and acoustic analysis. So we worked together, and I did not have to become an instant expert on respiratory physiology. One evening when Marcia and I were having dinner with Arend and Fenna Bouhuys and their friends in their New Haven home, I asked him if he knew anyone who knew anything about the anatomy of newborn babies.

The question may seem odd. Surely everything about human anatomy would have been discovered long ago and put into orderly books, profusely illustrated with diagrams and photographs. But I had been searching, without success, for detailed information on the tongue, mouth, and other vocal anatomy of newborn human infants for several months.

I had also been looking at the skulls of monkeys, chimpanzees, and newborn and adult humans and X-rays of their vocal tracts (the air passages above their larynges). It looked as though the human newborn airway was similar to those of apes and monkeys. Newborn infants' heads, moreover, didn't seem to look much like those of adults. In fact, they seemed to look somewhat like photographs of young monkeys and apes, absent hair. But no detailed anatomy book on newborn infants could I find. Arend asked why was I interested. I hesitantly told him that I had bought a plaster reproduction of the reconstructed skull of a Neanderthal man unearthed in the early part of the twentieth century in the French village of La Chapelle-aux-Saints. Though the massive Neanderthal skull with its brow ridge and protruding face did not really look human, it resembled a human newborn skull when you held it upside-down and looked at its bottom. And since the bottom of the skull supported the soft tissues of the newborn human airway, what could this tell us about the Neanderthal vocal tract and Neanderthal speech? But first I had to find out more about the relation between the skull and the muscles, cartilages, and soft tissue of the newborn infant's airway.

Arend's answer was both surprising and hopeful. The reason why I had not found a detailed anatomy book on newborn infants was that none had existed until that year—1969—and the author, the world's authority on the anatomy of newborn infants, was Ed Crelin, the chief of anatomy of the Yale University School of Medicine. On reflection, it was not too surprising that no one had until then produced a comprehensive study of this subject. Anatomy, like all aspects of medicine, has as its ultimate goal healing and the preservation of life. All books have intended audiences, and surgeons are the primary beneficiaries of anatomical studies. But surgery on infants was very risky until the 1960s and the advent of complex life-support systems that monitored heart rate, breathing, and blood pressure. The beeping monitors that are commonplace in both real operating rooms and those of TV dramas did not exist before then. Complex surgical procedures that lasted twelve hours or more could now be reasonably attempted. Surgery on infants, too, was now feasible under certain conditions. And since it was evident that infants are not just shrunken adults, surgeons wanted to know what they would find before attempting such surgery. Crelin had repeatedly been asked for information in emergencies, and it was clear to him that a comprehensive study of newborns' anatomy was needed.

Apart from the usual problems encountered in research, there was the difficulty of obtaining the bodies of infants. The death of a young child or infant is a tragic event, and to grieving parents the thought of their dead baby's body being methodically dissected is understandably horrific. But there was no other way to learn the anatomical details that might mean life or death for other babies. Crelin's *Anatomy of the Newborn: An Atlas* was the first book of its kind. Human newborn infants differ profoundly from normal adults.[1] The plump miniature adults who pass for babies in the paintings of the Italian Renaissance typify this mistaken view.

So on a Thursday afternoon I entered Crelin's anatomy laboratory with a small backpack stuffed with X-rays of supralaryngeal vocal tracts (SVTs), books showing the skulls of apes and monkeys, my research papers on the speech capabilities of monkeys and apes, and a plaster of Paris cast of the skull of the La Chapelle-aux-Saints Neanderthal adult male. The original fossil skull had been found in reasonably intact form and been pieced together in 1909 by Marcellin Boule, one of the great figures in biological anthropology, and was in a vault at the Musée de l'Homme in Paris. The plaster of Paris reproduction of Boule's reconstruction can still be bought from the Museum of Anthropology of the University of Pennsylvania and, as I confirmed when I checked it in 1972 against Boule's work in Paris, is an accurate copy.

Ed Crelin picked up the Neanderthal skull casting, turned it upside down, sideways, remarked on its size, and said, "He's a big baby."

Reconstructing the Vocal Tract

Muscles leave marks on bone. They are essentially "stitched" in place by fibers to particular parts of the bones. The principles that govern the way in which they are attached are virtually identical to the instructions that you'll find on the side of a container of glue or in a carpentry manual. Roughen the surface so that the glued fibers that anchor muscle will adhere to more surface area; attach parts on which more force will be exerted to larger surfaces. Therefore, when anatomists compare the muscles, ligaments, and other soft tissue with the bones and skulls to which they are attached, consistent relations are always apparent. Muscles that exert greater force when they contract are attached to bony surfaces that have become enlarged, dished out, roughened, or otherwise adapted to provide more surface area for the glued fibers that hold the muscle in place. For example, if you move your fingers down along the center of a friendly dog's head in a patting motion, you will feel the center point of a large crest, the upper edge of the attachment surface for the powerful temporalis muscles that help to close the dog's jaw. The surfaces into which the masseter muscles, which close the human jaws, are attached (anatomists use the term *inserted*) can be seen just above the cheekbones (the anatomical term for *cheekbone* is *zygomatic arch*). You can easily determine where these surfaces are located with your fingertips by feeling the masseter muscles contracting and releasing, as you open and close your jaws.

Comparative anatomical studies of the relations between muscles, ligaments, and the bones to which they attach show these consistent patterns. The positions and relative sizes of muscles as well as other soft tissue are reflected in the shape and relative proportions of bones and the surfaces, protuberances and hollows of the skull into which muscles and ligaments are inserted. In the course of evolution, natural selection generally produces reasonably good, though not always optimal, matches between bone and soft tissue. By using the known relations between the soft tissue and skeletal structure of newborn human infants and the similar aspects of the Neanderthal skull base (the bottom part of the skull that supports the soft tissue of the SVT, that is, the lips, tongue, pharynx, and so on), Crelin was able to make a reasonable attempt at reconstructing the Neanderthal vocal tract. New insights into the development of the human vocal tract in infants and children (which will be discussed in the next chapter) call for a reappraisal of Crelin's reconstruction, which probably places the Neanderthal vocal tract too close to that of a human newborn's. However, it is necessary to understand the principles that guided Crelin, because they form the starting point for the debate on Neanderthal speech capabilities and the evolution of human speech-producing anatomy. The illustrations from our 1971 paper, "On the Speech of Neanderthal Man," may make this clearer.

Perhaps the main reason why the similarities between human newborn skulls and Neanderthal skulls were not noted is their relative sizes. Figure as 3-1 shows typical newborn and adult human skulls and the La Chapelle-aux-Saints fossil skull scaled to about the same size. The newborn and Neanderthal skulls are more flattened from top to bottom and elongated. Their lower jaws are proportionately longer than those of adult humans, and they lack

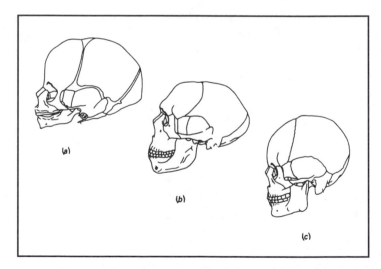

3-1—Lateral Views of Newborn, Neanderthal, and Adult Human Skulls
The skulls have been drawn to the same size. (a) newborn human infant skull, (b) La Chapelle-aux-Saints adult Neanderthal skull, (c) adult male human skull. (Adopted from Lieberman and Crelin 1971)

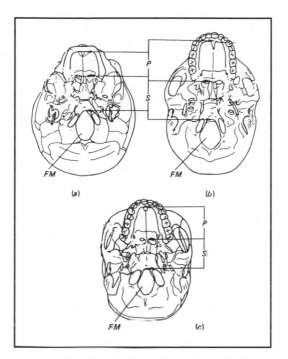

3-2—Bottom Views of Newborn, Neanderthal, and Adult Human Skulls
The skulls have been drawn to the same size. (*a*) newborn human infant skull, (*b*)
La Chapelle-aux-Saints adult Neanderthal skull, (*c*) adult male human skull. The
position of the foramen magnum (FM) is marked on each skull, as well as the
length of the palate (P) and the distance (S) between the end of the palate and
foramen magnum. Note the relatively long distance S on the Neanderthal and
newborn skulls. (Adopted from Lieberman and Crelin, 1971)

chins. The newborn and Neanderthal faces project in front of the
upper part of the skull that encloses the frontal regions of the
brain. This projection is more pronounced in the Neanderthal
skull and is one of the characteristics that differentiate Neanderthals from modern humans.

Figure 3-2 shows the inferior (bottom) views of the same three
skulls. The bottom of the skull supports the SVT, and the newborn
and Neanderthal skulls show striking similarities. The hard palate is
the bony structure that forms the roof of the front of your mouth;

you can easily feel it with your fingers. Behind the hard palate is an area extending from the back of the hard palate to the point at which the spinal column joins with the skull at the foramen magnum (literally, the big hole). The opening to the nose is located in this area. One of the keys to understanding how the Neanderthal supralaryngeal airway can be reconstructed is the distance between the end of the hard palate and the foramen magnum. In newborn infants this distance is as long as, or slightly longer than, the length of the palate. It has to be long because the larynx in a newborn is positioned close to the opening to the nose, with the pharynx (a soft-tissue structure that in infants propels food and liquid down the digestive system) positioned behind the larynx. Note the long distance between the forward edge of the foramen magnum and the forward edge of the hard palate. This skeletal feature reflects the long Neanderthal mouth. You can see the geometry of the inside space of the adult and newborn mouth, larynx, and pharynx and Crelin's Neanderthal reconstruction in the photograph to the right.

The space inside anyone's mouth, larynx, and pharynx is hard to visualize. Conventional X-rays can show a cross-sectional view, but not the volume. Crelin used a technique similar to the one used to cast bronze statues: if you can make a mold that wraps around the space that defines some object, then you can make a "casting" of the object by pouring into the mold some material that will fill up the mold, conforming to its inner shape and then setting. Sculptors often carve a statue in wax and then place clay over the finished wax statue to form a mold. Molten bronze can then be poured into the wax-filled mold. The molten bronze will, of course, melt the wax and fill the mold; the bronze cools down and solidifies to form the finished statue.

The actual supralaryngeal airways of newborn and adult human cadavers served as "molds" for the castings shown in this photograph. The cadavers were first frozen and then sectioned in half along a front-to-back midline. The shape and position of the tongue was then checked against X-rays of living adults saying the sound *uh* (the phonetic "schwa" or "neutral" vowel), and X-ray movies of newborn infants were taken while they cried aloud and swallowed.

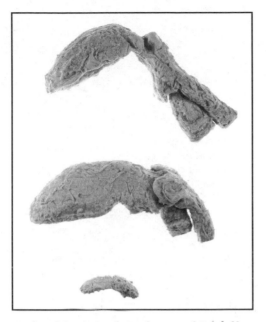

3-3—Photographs of Castings of Newborn and Adult Human SVTs
Casts of the supralaryngeal vocal tracts, including the nasal airway, of (*top*) an adult male human, (*middle*) Edmund S. Crelin's reconstruction of the La Chapelle-aux-Saints adult male Neanderthal, and (*bottom*) a newborn human.

This step was necessary because soft tissue can become distorted after death and during the processes used to prepare cadavers for anatomical studies. Liquid silicone rubber was placed into the two half-sectioned larynx, mouth, and pharyngeal cavities. The silicone rubber half sections were removed after they had set and were glued together. I had used a similar method the year before to obtain a casting of the supralaryngeal airways of a rhesus monkey.

You can see the different shape, positions, and proportions of the newborn and adult human supralaryngeal airways in the photographs and sketches. In the newborn the larynx is positioned close to the bottom of the skull. Independent X-ray studies by Jeffrey Laitman and Edmund Crelin at Yale University and by James Bosma at the National Institutes of Health in Bethesda, Maryland, X-ray

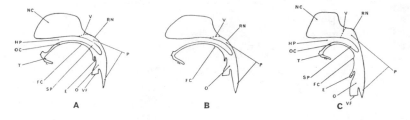

3-4—Lateral Views of SVTs

Supralaryngeal vocal tracts scaled to same size of (*a*) a newborn human, (*b*) the 1971 reconstruction of the La Chapelle-aux-Saints adult male Neanderthal, and (*c*) an adult male human. The keyed symbols are as follows: NC = nasal cavity, V = vomer bone, which divides the nasal cavity in two, RN = roof of the nasopharynx, P = pharynx, HP = hard palate (the bony "roof" of the mouth), SP = soft palate, or velum, OC = oral cavity, T = tip of the tongue (often confused with the entire tongue), FC = foramen cecum of tongue, E = epiglottis, O = opening of larynx into pharynx, VF = the level of the vocal cords, or "folds" (the two terms are synonymous). (After Lieberman and Crelin 1971)

movies made in Stockholm (by Hank Truby, James Bosma, and John Lind in 1965, before the long-term effects of radiation were appreciated), and subsequent studies show that when newborn infants breathe and drink, they pull their larynx up and seal it into firm contact with the opening to their nose in the space between the end of the roof of their mouth (the hard palate) and the foramen magnum. The newborn pharynx is positioned *behind*, almost in line with, the larynx. The long distance between the end of the hard palate (about 2.6 cm on the average) reflects the anatomical fact that there has to be room for a larynx positioned close to the base of the skull with the pharynx behind it. The length of the newborn larynx is about 2.0 cm, leaving room for it to be positioned almost in line with the tongue so that it can lock into the nose.

Looking at the newborn supralaryngeal airway, we can see that the relatively small newborn larynx can rise, like a submarine's periscope, through the mouth cavity and lock into the nose (in the region termed the nasopharynx), leaving room on either side of it for liquid and small particles of food to pass into the pharynx. The pharynx has a set of powerful constrictor muscles that propel the ingested material back and down into the stomach. Therefore, newborn infants can simultaneously breathe and suckle without the danger of choking on liquid entering the larynx. The newborn human breathing-eating arrangement is the "standard plan" for all present-day mammals, except normal human beings over the age of three months or so, when the larynx begins to descend down into the pharynx.[2] It takes about fifteen years for the larynx to reach its final low position; the process involves both the differential growth of the tongue and pharynx and the restructuring of the bones of the skull. However, a recent reanalysis of a series of X-rays that reveal the development of the vocal tract and skull in infants and children from the age of three months onward shows that the pharynx and mouth cavities of the human vocal tract reach their adult proportions at about the age of seven years (McCarthy and D. Lieberman in press).[3]

The image in Figure 3-5 shows the oral supralaryngeal airway of an adult man derived from a cineradiographic (X-ray) motion picture in which his head was carefully positioned to avoid a distorted image. The larynx has moved down into the neck, below the pharynx in adult humans. Therefore, there doesn't have to be room for these structures in the space between the back of the hard palate and the foramen magnum. That's what Edmund Crelin and I found to be the case in adult human skulls. This distance was shorter than the length of the palate (5.1 cm average, range 4.6–5.7 cm) in forty-eight of fifty adult skulls, measuring, on the average, 4.1 cm (range 3.6–4.9 cm). In two adult human skulls it was slightly longer (0.4 cm), and in the other exceptional case both dimensions were 4.6 cm long. The length of the adult human male larynx ranges between 3.5 and 4.5 cm, which would leave no room for the soft palate if it occupied the standard-plan position, close to the base of the skull. Earlier independent studies of human skulls, such as one of Lapp and Norwegian skulls by the Norwegian orthodontist Olav Bergland in 1963, had yielded similar metrical data. This is, of course, what anatomists usually expect to find—a consistent anatomical relation between the skull and nearby soft-tissue structures.

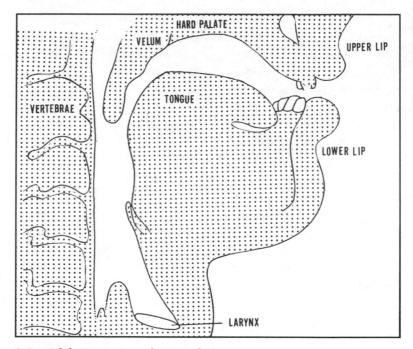

3-5— Adult Human Supralaryngeal Airway

A sketch of the supralaryngeal vocal tract (SVT) of an adult human derived from cineradiographic views of a living subject. Note the shape and relative size of the human tongue. It is often distorted and reduced in size in the illustrations of many anatomy texts, which apparently reprint anatomical dissections of cadavers without checking them against X-rays or MRIs of living subjects. The ability of the human SVT to produce the sounds [i], [u], and [a] derives from the fact that the tongue body moving as a whole can produce abrupt changes in the cross-sectional area of the supralaryngeal airway at the junction of the oral and pharyngeal cavities. It would be impossible either to swallow or to talk if the entire tongue were removed.

In contrast, the Neanderthal skull shows that it could have supported a larynx positioned closer to the base on the skull. The distance between the palate and the foramen magnum is 6.2 cm, well outside the range of any of the hundreds of human skulls measured by William Howells at Harvard's Peabody Museum of Anthropology. Howells, the world's leading authority on skull measurements, has over the course of forty years measured and published studies of human populations throughout the world.[4] There would be ample room for a Neanderthal larynx positioned close to the base of the La Chapelle-aux-Saints fossil skull even if this larynx were as large as (4.5 cm long) or somewhat larger than the largest measured adult human male larynges. Similar conclusions were reached in an independent study by Clotilde Grosmangin, who worked in Paris with the original La Chapelle-aux-Saints Neanderthal skull and the slightly different La Ferrassie I Neanderthal skull. In fact, an earlier reconstruction of a Neanderthal supralaryngeal airway by Sir Arthur Keith and Victor Negus had come to a similar conclusion. However, except for a sketch published in Negus's 1949 summary of his anatomical studies, no details were published; my attempts to discover the details twenty years later were fruitless.

What Couldn't Neanderthals Say?

It is clearly impossible to look at the head and neck of a living human being and state what language he or she speaks. Nor will detailed anatomical measurements of the SVT resolve this question. But the negative question can be answered in some instances. The victims of certain developmental anomalies that produce malformed SVTs inherently cannot produce certain sounds. Karen Landahl, a linguist at the University of Chicago,[5] and Herbert Gould of the Center for Craniofacial Anomalies in Chicago, for example, found that Apert's syndrome results in malformed SVTs that are unable to produce sounds like the vowels [i] and [u] (the vowels of *see* and *Sue* or *bee* and *boo*—English spelling isn't consistent). On reading this, you might reasonably wonder whether this speech deficit might be caused by motor control problems rather than by the anatomy of their SVTs. Landahl solved this problem by using the same method that Dennis Klatt,[6] Ed Crelin, Katherine Harris, William Wilson, and I used to determine the speech-producing limits of monkey, ape, newborn, and Neanderthal vocal tracts. The method is simple. The formant frequencies that specify vowels and other speech sounds are simply the frequencies at which maximal acoustic energy will pass through the vocal tract; they are determined by the shape and length of the vocal tract. Therefore, we can determine the range of sounds that a particular vocal tract can produce.

The most direct way of doing this would be to first hammer out a brass tube that has a shape as close as possible to that necessary to produce the formant frequencies of a particular speech sound. The next step would be to attach the mouthpiece and reed of a clarinet to the end of the tube, blow through the mouthpiece and listen. Since, as the previous chapter noted, the physiology of human speech production is similar to the way in which woodwinds work, this procedure is appropriate (formant frequencies are equivalent to the "resonances" of the musical instrument). This is, in fact, the method that Kratzenstein, a descendant of the German scholars invited to Russia by Tsar Peter the Great, used in 1780 when he was awarded a prize by the Academy of Sciences of St. Petersburg for synthesizing the vowels of Russian. However, we instead used computers rather than hammered brass.

Computer programs that calculate the formant frequencies produced by a given SVT have a number of applications that transcend "pure" research. They can be used to produce artificial speech for interactive computer systems and for long-range speech systems that could be useful for space travel in the next century (the systems compress the frequency band necessary for preserving the intelligibility of speech, thereby conserving transmitter power). Bill Henke's dissertation research at MIT had produced a system that calculated with great precision the formant frequencies that any given SVT shape generated. Dennis Klatt and I sat down before the computer housed in Building 20, a rambling wooden building rapidly thrown together at the start of World War II in a secret project to develop military radars. Fortunately, in light of new data indicating that the Neanderthal vocal tract probably was more developed than a newborn's, Edmund Crelin had purposely adopted a conservative position and "given" the Neanderthal a more humanlike vocal tract than a newborn's. We systematically entered all the shapes that the reconstructed Neanderthal vocal tract could make to cover the known range of vowels that characterizes all human languages. Vowel production is governed by the position of the tongue, lips, and larynx. We were guided by X-ray studies of the shapes that adult and newborn humans actually produce. X-ray movies of many languages had been produced at Haskins Laboratories; still X-rays of speakers of other languages had been produced at laboratories in the United States, Europe, and Japan. We also took into account basic physiological and acoustic constraints; the limits on how sharp a bend a tongue can make, the maximum constriction that can be produced without producing noisy turbulent nonvowel air flow. When in doubt, we allowed acrobatic maneuvers aimed at producing the vowels [i], [u], and [a], the "universal" vowels used by virtually all human languages. These vowels also delimit the total range of vowels that any normal human can produce. We modeled adult and newborn human vocal tracts using the same procedure.

The formant frequencies generated by the computer model for the newborn and adult vocal tracts matched acoustic analyses, so we knew that the general procedure was working. The Neanderthal vocal tract could produce virtually all human vowels *except* [i], [u], and [a]. It also couldn't produce consonants like [k] and [g], the initial consonants of *cod* and *god*. Moreover, all the speech sounds that it produced would have had a nasal quality. Similar limits apply to the newborn supralaryngeal airway and to monkey and chimpanzee SVTs.

So What Do Neanderthal Speech Limits Mean?

The significance of *not* being able to say [i] was not fully apparent to us, and its full understanding required much additional work by many other people. The eminent scholar Roman Jakobson, who had revitalized American linguistics when he arrived in New York after fleeing from the Nazi invasion of Prague, had pointed out that all human languages used vowels like [i], [u], and [a]. Most languages also used other vowels, but these three were always present. We also knew that the vowel [i] was most resistant to confusion. Tests of the confusability of vowels at Bell Telephone Laboratories (now Lucent Technology), directed by Gordon Peterson, one of the world's most prominent speech scientists, had yielded some puzzling results. The Bell system was in 1952 beginning to develop devices that could recognize human speech, and researchers wanted to know how accurate human listeners would be if they had to identify a single word spoken by an unknown speaker. Peterson devised a clever experiment. He first had seventy-six speakers read lists of words having the form hVd—for example, *heed, had, hop*. The speakers included adult males and females and teenage children. The words produced by the different speakers were then grouped in ten-speaker blocks and scrambled so that a person listening to a tape recording prepared in this manner wouldn't know what the next word on the list was, nor would the speaker necessarily be the same speaker. When large groups of listeners were asked to write down the words they heard on these tape recordings, unexpectedly high error rates occurred for practically all the vowels except [i] and, to a lesser degree, [u]. In ten thousand trials [i] was confused two times. Words with the vowel [u] had six confusions. Five hundred or more confusions occurred for words that used other vowels; for example, *hit* would be confused with *head*.

At about the same time, Peter Ladefoged, who went on to establish a center for speech research at UCLA, working with the psychologist Donald Broadbent in Cambridge, England, showed that people's phonetic judgments took into account the length of the vocal tract that had produced the speech signal they were "perceiving." Ladefoged and Broadbent first used a speech synthesizer (a pre–computer age "analog" machine that converted formant frequency patterns and other cues into artificial speech) to produce the unfinished sentence "The word that you will hear is . . ." Three versions of the sentence were produced, corresponding to a person with a long vocal tract, to one with a short vocal tract, and to one with a midlength vocal tract. The words *bit, bat,* and *but* corresponding to the midlength vocal tract were also synthesized. When these words were placed at the end of the midlength carrier, they were correctly identified by a panel of listeners who were all native speakers of British English. However, the same listeners heard the tape-recorded *but* as *bat* and the tape-recorded *bat* as *bit* when these tape-recorded words were heard at the end of the long vocal tract carrier. The listeners' phonetic perception of the tape-recorded words also shifted when they were heard after the short vocal tract carrier sentence; the tape-recorded *bit* went to *bat,* and the tape-recorded *bat* to *but.* The same acoustic signals were being heard as different vowels when they were preceded by carrier sentences that led the listeners to believe that they had been produced by speakers who had different vocal tract lengths. Ladefoged and Broadbent correctly concluded that human listeners, at some unconscious level, took into account the length of a person's vocal tract when they "decoded" the complex formant frequency patterns that specify the sounds of human speech.

But we don't generally have to wait for a second or two to comprehend a spoken word. How can we understand anything if we always have to estimate the speaker's vocal tract length? The key to the puzzle was discovered in 1978 by Terrance Nearey, who now heads a speech research group at the University of Alberta, in Canada. Subsequent studies by Björn Lindblom and his colleagues at the University of Stockholm and others in Japan, the United States, and the United Kingdom replicated Nearey's work. What occurs when we interpret speech signals is a "normalization" process in which we can seize on a number of different cues that allow us to estimate the probable length of the vocal tract of the person who's talking to us. We are not aware of this process. In essence the normalization process is similar to the way we unconsciously take into account the size of the image formed on our retina when we recognize the face of a person or the shape of an object. Human listeners make use of many cues to normalize the speech signals that they hear. But Nearey and Lindblom independently showed that the vowel [i] is the most reliable cue for this process. The explanation hinges on the fact that the human vocal tract is being pushed to extreme limits when anyone says [i]; [u] offers the second-best clue for normalization. For other vowels, alternative maneuvers can produce the effect of a vocal tract longer or shorter than that which actually characterizes a particular speaker.

Other studies in the late 1970s affirmed what speech clinicians had known for many years. Nasalization of speech lowers its intelligibility; Zivi Bond showed that the error rate doubled when speech signals were nasalized. It becomes much harder to unscramble the formant frequency patterns that count, because of the interference created by the formants and other acoustic effects that occur when the soft palate (positioned at the rear, posterior end of the hard palate) is lowered, opening the nasal airway as you speak. In the case of newborn, primate, and the reconstructed Neanderthal vocal tracts, the soft palate inherently cannot isolate the nasal airway from the mouth and pharynx.

However, these speech deficiencies do *not* mean that Neanderthals did not talk or that they did not possess language. It was apparent in 1971 that the phonetic deficits of Neanderthal hominids did not preclude their having speech and language. The stone tools that have been found with Neanderthal remains are complex. They were clothed and used fires in a controlled manner. The La Chapelle-aux-Saints fossil that we studied had suffered from arthritis, had lost most of his teeth years before he died, and clearly was a member of a society that cared for the infirm. Neanderthal speech-producing anatomy could have produced almost all of the speech sounds that occur in human languages. However, they could not have produced sounds like [i] and [u], which are most resistant to confusion and which furnish useful clues to the length of a speaker's vocal tract. These sounds enhance the robustness of human speech in noisy environments—the normal state of affairs in which we must unscramble the speech signal of the person to whom we are listening from competing voices and environmental noise. And, as we'll see, our ancestors were equipped to produce these sounds and may have had brains that were better adapted for speech, language, and higher cognition because of their enhanced speech production ability.

CHAPTER 4

Dead Men and Women Talk Again

LOST IN THE HEATED debate about Neanderthal speech was the fact that despite their deficits, Neanderthals surely talked to each other in some form of language or "protolanguage." Unlike present-day chimpanzees, which cannot produce even voluntary modifications of their cries, Neanderthals undoubtedly had brains that would have allowed them to talk.

"Paleoneurology"

The evidence that this is the case clearly doesn't derive from any direct detailed knowledge of the Neanderthal brain. The last Neanderthals died about 30,000 years ago, so no vestige of their brain tissue survives. However, because their skulls have survived, the size of their brains can be estimated. The volume of Neanderthal brains ranged from 1,200 to 1,750 cc, about the same (1,200 to 1,700 cc) range as that of early and present specimens of modern *Homo sapiens*. This doesn't mean that they were as clever as modern human beings, since brain size is also related to muscularity and climatic conditions. People who live in colder climates tend to have larger brains, and Neanderthals lived in Eurasia during a cold period. Neanderthal skeletal bones also show that they were massive. They had short, stocky bodies; males probably weighed about 145 pounds and stood less than five feet seven inches tall. Brain volume also is correlated with heavier massive muscles and body weight in closely related species. Heinz Stephan, a German neuroanatomist, has been studying the sizes of the brains and their various parts in many species over the past forty years. His detailed measurements show that bigger muscles require bigger brains, independent of intelligence.

But brain tissue is expensive in biological terms, and Neanderthal brains are large even when we factor in the probable muscle mass. Stephan's data, for example, indicate that the Neanderthal brain is four times larger than that of a 105-kg gorilla. Stephan's studies, which are confirmed by other comparative studies—most notably by those of Harry Jerrison at UCLA, one of the world's leading authorities on brain evolution—show that if you take into account the body weight of related species, bigger brains roughly correlate with more "intelligent" behavior. So we can conclude that Neanderthal hominids, though they would make superb football linebackers, were not gorillas. But how clever were they?

Detailed knowledge of the shape and proportions of the Neanderthal brain might shed more light on their language and thinking abilities, but this again entails finding an intact brain. Some anthropologists have attempted to determine the language capacity of Neanderthal and other hominid fossil brains by looking at the marks left on the insides of the fossil skulls. The folds and ridges that divide various parts of the outermost layer of the primate brain, the "neocortex," sometimes leave faint markings on the inside of the skull. If you examine an "endocast," an impression of the inside surface of the reconstructed skull of a fossil, you can see these faint markings. Dean Falk, an anthropologist at the State University of New York at Albany, and linguists such as Wendy Wilkins and Jennie Wakefield at the University of Arizona have claimed that these traces show that certain fossil hominids possessed human language. These claims rest on the traditional model of the human brain's language capacity.

In the second half of the nineteenth century the French neurologist Paul Broca studied a man who lost various aspects of language after his brain was damaged by a massive stroke. The patient had extreme difficulty in speaking and writing and was paralyzed on the right side of his body. Though a large part of this man's brain was destroyed, Broca claimed that one small, localized area in the front part of the left side of his neocortex was the "seat" of expressive language. Later studies of *aphasia*, the destruction of language and speech after brain damage, identified a second area toward the back of the left side of the neocortex, Wernicke's area, which was thought to be related to problems that people had in comprehending the meanings of words after brain damage.

Broca's and Wernicke's areas are traditionally supposed to be *the* parts of the human brain that confer language. However, as we will see in the next chapter, the traditional theory is wrong. Many other structures, some of them deep within the brain, are implicated in language. It wasn't really possible to test the traditional theory until the advent of brain imaging techniques such as computerized tomography (CT) and magnetic resonance imaging (MRI), which reveal the true extent of damage from strokes. The research of the past two decades shows, beyond any reasonable doubt, that deep subcortical neuroanatomical structures and pathways are implicated in language and thinking. Regions of the neocortex, the outer layer of the human brain, in the general vicinity of Broca's and Wernicke's areas, do play a part in regulating human language. However, complex pathways linking subcortical and neocortical regions are the bases of human language and thinking. We will later discuss this research, which links the evolution of human linguistic and cognitive ability to brain mechanisms that probably first evolved to make rapid motor responses to sensory information.

What is germane to the question of Neanderthal cleverness is that we would not be able to say much about the linguistic capacities of a Neanderthal or any other hominid's brain, even if we could somehow look at its intact neocortical surface. Moreover, it is doubtful that endocasts reveal the neocortical surfaces of fossil brains. The problem is the faint, uncertain nature of the endocast markings. As Ralph Holloway of Columbia University, who has studied fossil brain endocasts for more than two decades, notes in commenting on Wilkins and Wakefield's (1994) attempt to infer language from endocasts, "Bluntly, the ugly fact is that there is not one single well-documented instance of paleoneurological evidence that unambiguously demonstrates a relative expansion of the parietal-occipital-temporal junction [Broca's and Wernicke's areas and hypothetical connections] in early *Homo*" (Holloway 1995, 191). In fact, given our present knowledge (or ignorance) of how brains work, any fine-grained assessment of the linguistic or cognitive abilities of another species must be based on observations of overt behavior. This is clearly so when we attempt to assess the intelligence of individual human beings; the only way of determining the intelligence or linguistic skills of individuals (excluding people who have suffered brain damage) is to see and hear what they can do. An MRI or CT scan, even direct observation of the brain after death, is useless. In the case of our early hominid ancestors, we can make some general inferences on the basis of overall volume and weight of their brains, but we must rely on the archaeological record to get some idea of what they could do. And the imperfect archaeological record is difficult to assess.

The Chronology of Hominid Evolution

Although anthropologists differ on the details, the general model of hominid evolution is not in dispute. About five million years ago common ancestors of apes and humans lived. The fossil remains of this hypothetical common ancestral species have not yet been found. Present-day apes and hominids (primates in or closely related to our line of descent) that had some of the "derived" anatomical features that differentiate us from apes, evolved from this common ancestor. The date of the split was first established by geneticists who compared the DNA of humans with that of chimpanzees. Some parts of the genetic DNA code that do not contribute to biological fitness gradually mutate, slowly changing over the course of time. The rate of change for these "neutral" aspects of the DNA code is known, so it is possible to calculate the approximate time at which this momentous (for us) event occurred.[1]

Recent fossil finds are consistent with both the approximate date and the probable resemblance of present-day chimpanzees to our common ancestor. In September 1995, Maeve Leakey, the wife of Richard Leakey, who is the most prominent active member of the Leakey fossil-hunting dynasty, discovered a 4.1-million-year-old hominid fossil near Lake Turkana, in Kenya, which belongs to a species that she named *Australopithecus anamensis*. The fossil's arm and leg bones showed that it walked bipedally. The 3.6-million-year-old *Australopithecus afarensis* fossils unearthed in Ethiopia, the best-known being the skeleton that Donald Johanson of the Institute for Human Origins in Berkeley named Lucy, likewise were adapted for upright bipedal walking, but they also had small brains. The oldest hominid fossil that has yet been found is the 4.4-million-year-old one that Tim White, a paleontologist at the University of California at Berkeley, and his colleagues found in 1995 and named *Ardipithecus ramidus*. The volume of the brains of various australopithecine species ranges between 350 and 530 cc, not much larger than the 400-cc brain of a present-day chimpanzee weighing 45 kg. What seems to be most significant is the multiplicity of early hominid species. As Maeve Leakey put it, "You never get a novel adaptation like bipedalism without a radiation of species, a number of experiments in this adaptation." In other words, there is no simple evolutionary sequence that leads from the common ape-hominid ancestor to us. Every new fossil find seems to turn up another evolutionary "new-model hominid," and most of these experiments ultimately became extinct, edged out by a slightly better adapted, newer model. As Charles Darwin noted,

> any variation, however slight and from whatever cause pro-
> ceeding, if it be in any degree profitable to an individual of any
> species, in its infinitely complex relations to organic beings
> and external nature will tend to the preservation of that indi-
> vidual and will generally be inherited by its offspring. The off-
> spring, also, will have a better chance of surviving, for of the
> many members of a species which are periodically born but a
> small number can survive. I have called this principle, by
> which each small variation if useful is preserved by the term of
> Natural Selection. (Darwin 1859, 61)

The heated debates over which fossils define different australopithecine species and which species are in our direct line of
descent may surprise people outside the field. The Leakeys, Mary,
Richard, and Maeve, have been barely on speaking terms with Tim
White and Donald Johanson. But theories concerning human
evolution and what makes humans distinctive always stir up feelings that would be absent if the debate were instead about pigs or
horses.[2]

The later stages of hominid evolution also appear to have taken
place in Africa. About 2 million years ago hominids with 500- to
800-cc brains, almost twice the size of a chimpanzee's, appear in the
fossil record. These fossils—sometimes placed into one species
called *Homo habilis*, sometimes divided into two different species—
were also better adapted for bipedal locomotion. Some *Homo habilis*
or *Homo erectus* groups (the issue is unresolved) migrated across Asia
to western China. The next generally accepted "level" is marked by
the appearance of *Homo erectus* about 1.9 million years ago with a
brain volume ranging from 750 to 1,250 cc, depending on which
particular fossils are placed within the species. Fossils unearthed
throughout Europe and Asia show that *Homo erectus* hominids left
Africa and established themselves on the landmasses that they could
reach on foot.[3] Neanderthals are considered by many anthropolo-

gists to be a species derived from *Homo erectus* about 300,000 to 150,000 years ago. The "classic" Neanderthals fossils that were discovered in the late nineteenth century and the early twentieth derived from Neanderthals living in western Europe, but Neanderthal fossils have since been recovered in western Asia (the Mideast) and in other sites as far east as Teshik-Tash, in Uzbekistan.

The Archaeological Record

The earliest reliably dated archaeological evidence that can shed light on the brains of early hominids dates to about 2.4 million years ago, the time of the australopithecines. Though some undated stone tools may be older, Oldowan tools have been found in many sites in Africa that can be dated to between 2.4 and 1.5 million years ago. Various methods that take into account such factors as the decay rates of radioactive elements, the changing magnetic field of the planet, and the age of the remains of extinct animals and plants found with the tools are used to date stone tools as well as fossils. New methods are continually being introduced, and the ages of particular fossils and tools often change dramatically as more refined dating procedures are introduced. The name Oldowan refers to one of the sites at which these tools were first found, the Olduvai Gorge, in Tanzania. However, similar tools radiometrically dated to the same era have been unearthed in Kenya and Ethiopia; similar ones that probably are about the same age have been found as far north as Casablanca and in South Africa. Oldowan tools are simple. Figure 4-1 shows a few examples.

However, though they are simple, crude tools by modern standards, it is not so simple to make them. As Nicholas Toth and Kathy Schick of Indiana University, who have themselves mastered the art of stone tool making, point out,

> some important principles of flaking stone tools had been mastered by two million years ago. These include (a) the ability to recognize acute angles on cores [the piece of stone from

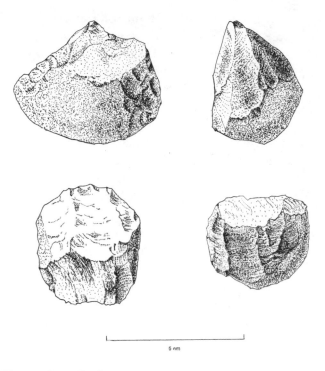

5 nm

4-1—Oldowan Stone Tools
Stone tools from the lowest, hence earliest, levels excavated by Mary Leakey at
Olduvai Gorge. (Adapted from Leakey 1971)

which a tool is flaked off] to serve as striking platforms from
which to detach flakes and fragments, and (b) good hand-eye
coordination when flaking stone, including the dexterity to
strike the core with a hammerstone with a sharp, glancing
blow. It would appear that a strong power grip, as well as a
strong precision grip, was characteristic of early hominid toolmaking populations at this time. (Toth and Schick 1993, 349)

Randall Susman, a biological anthropologist at the State University of New York at Stony Brook, has presented convincing evidence that some of the australopithecines who lived during this

period possessed another derived human feature, fingers that like ours are adapted to precise, forceful manual activity—the human "power grip." The anatomy that facilitates the kind of manual action involved in wood carving or making a stone tool seems to have evolved in these early hominids. Thus there is evidence for a "match" between brain and body. Natural selection that retained small variations enhancing an individual's ability to execute the skilled manual maneuvers needed to make stone tools would place a higher adaptive value on variations that enhanced the brainpower necessary to coordinate one's hand, arm, and body, enabling one to strike a powerful, precise blow. It is impossible to state which came first, adaptations that enhanced brainpower or the finger anatomy, but the net process would characterize what engineers term "positive feedback"—brain and body evolving together to achieve a goal that enhanced survival and the survival of offspring. However, we can infer the presence of the brain mechanisms that enabled these fossils to make stone tools, from the fact that their anatomy was adapted to this end. Anatomy that can be read in the fossil record, therefore, can be used as a key to the puzzle of brain evolution.

Nicholas Toth provided other clues to the brains and cognitive abilities of early hominids. Toth first learned to make stone tools so that he could see what was involved. It became apparent that the materials used to produce Oldowan tools had to be transported over fairly long distances. Chimpanzees have not been observed transporting material for toolmaking, so this may imply a degree of planning that transcends that shown by chimpanzees. Toth also believes that the pattern by which flakes are chipped away shows that Oldowan tools were made by right-handed individuals. Toth is right-handed. He found that fracture marks similar to those of Oldowan tools were produced when he held the stone with his left hand and hammered away with another stone held in his dominant right hand. (He also had to protect his legs with a thick leather apron, another technical necessity implying forethought.) So we can infer that the hominids who made similar stone tools were right-handed and planned ahead, but it is not clear whether australopithecine or *Homo erectus* hominids made them.

Tools, Brain Lateralization, and Language

Brain lateralization has often been equated with the human brain's language capabilities as well as with handedness. The brain is divided, front to back, into two hemispheres, each of which seems to be more involved in regulating particular activities. Brains appear to parcel out some activities to either the right or the left side of the brain. Human language and precise manual motor control are among the activities that are "lateralized." The lateralized structures of the brain that regulate language and handedness are usually opposite to that of the dominant hand, and 90 percent of us have dominant left brain hemispheres that control both precise manual maneuvers and language. However, it is also clear that brain lateralization is a "primitive," phylogenetically ancient character that, in itself, does not indicate that an animal possesses language. It has been evident since the 1970s that the more complex aspects of birdsong are also regulated by the dominant (usually the left) hemisphere of bird brains, but birds don't have language. Richard Bauer surprised most neurophysiologists when he found that the vocalizations of frogs are regulated by one hemisphere of their brains. Bauer's 1993 paper is generally ignored by linguists and psychologists who believe that the lateralization of the human brain is somehow the key to language. His frog study explains why both birds and mammals that evolved from different reptiles have lateralized brains. Brain lateralization already existed in the ancestors of birds and mammals.

Many mammals show signs of brain lateralization. Individual mice, for example, show paw preferences, although the mouse species as a whole isn't right-pawed or left-pawed. Victor Denenberg, a distinguished ethological psychologist at the University of

Connecticut, showed that some mice were left-pawed and some right-pawed. Denenberg placed a mouse in a cage that had a small hole in its floor through which only one paw would pass. Below the hole a granola-honey mixture was within reach of the extended paw. The mouse consistently used one paw to reach through the hole and scoop up the treat. Some mice consistently used their right paw; others used their left paw. Some families of mice tended to be right-pawed and others left-pawed. Denenberg in a 1981 review of brain lateralization in animals noted many other examples in which one hemisphere, or the other, of the brain regulated the direction in which they ran on "running-wheels," left-right movements, and birdsong. Most species do not show a general propensity for left or right lateralization. For that matter, it is obvious that human language cannot depend on having a *left* dominant hemisphere. Although about 90 percent of the human population is right-handed, which usually correlates with the left hemisphere of the brain's being more involved in language processing, that still leaves millions of people who use their right hemisphere for language processing. About all that we can conclude from the fact that 90 percent of us are left-hemisphere language and hand dominant is that human beings are the descendants of an australopithecine-like family whose members were predominantly right-handed some five million years ago.

About 1.5 million years ago a second "stage" of tools appeared at about the same time as the emergence of *Homo erectus* fossils. The products of this Lower Paleolithic industry are far more complex than Oldowan tools. The symmetrical forms shown in Figure 4-2 have straight or smoothed edges, which require great stone-cutting skills. Modern human toolmakers have to practice for months before they can master Lower Paleolithic techniques. However, though Lower Paleolithic tools gradually became more refined, there is a curious lack of change over time. The Mousterian tool technology associated with Neanderthal and early modern human hominids is regarded by some specialists as an extension of Lower Paleolithic techniques. Ian Davidson and William Noble, in fact, argue that toolmaking techniques were static until about

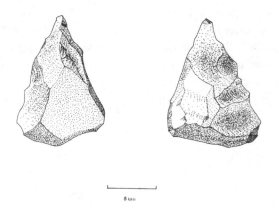

5 cm

4-2—Lower Paleolithic Stone Tools

Early Lower Paleolithic handaxes excavated in India. They are dated to a period approximately 700,000 years ago and demonstrate the toolmaking abilities of the archaic hominids who migrated into the Indian subcontinent. Similar tools are found in Africa, Europe, and Asia. (Adapted from Mishra et al. 1995)

35,000 years ago, when modern human beings completely replaced *Homo erectus* and Neanderthals. Davidson and Noble ascribe the sudden appearance of bone needles, polished stone tools, ornaments, sculpture, and paintings to fully developed human cognitive and linguistic ability. But their conclusions are much too strong because (a) Middle Paleolithic toolmaking technologies such as the Mousterian in fact differ substantially from earlier Lower Paleolithic techniques and (b) material culture doesn't equate in any direct way with brainpower.

Some general inferences concerning cognitive and linguistic ability can be drawn from the archaeological stone tool record. Lower Paleolithic tools clearly are more refined than Oldowan tools. Lower Paleolithic techniques seem to be beyond the capacity of any chimpanzee; many humans would have problems making these tools, and it is possible that only skilled *Homo erectus* specialists made them. The long, million-year static period noted by Davidson, Noble, and many other scholars may reflect the absence of the innovative bent of the modern human brain. However, there are obvious dangers in linking toolmaking technology directly to brain development. As Jonathan Kingdon points out in his insightful book *Self-Made Man*, Oldowan tools were still being made and used by modern human beings in some parts of the world as late as the nineteenth century. They did the job and were easy to make. Kingdon also points out the cognitive significance of another technology—fire. *Homo erectus* made extensive use of fires, apparently for driving animals toward hunters as well as for roasting meat. Controlled fires were employed in *Homo erectus* sites where the remains of hearths have been found. *Homo erectus* clearly possessed manual, cognitive, and probably language abilities commensurate with increased brain size. As we shall see in the next chapter, the brain bases regulating manual, cognitive, and linguistic ability are to some degree linked, so we can make some general, though not detailed, inferences concerning language and thought from the archaeological tool record.

Symbolic Tools and Early Modern Humans

The first reasonably complete fossils that can positively be identified as having modern human anatomy lived between 150,000 and 100,000 years ago on the southern rim of the Mediterranean Sea. They probably were part of the migration of modern humans out of Africa; earlier, incomplete African fossils have some of the derived features that differentiate modern human beings from the *Homo erectus* populations that they displaced (the displaced Neanderthals in many ways appear to be a specialized *Homo erectus* descendant). Although the stone tools of these early modern human beings did not differ from those found with Neanderthals, their interactions with nature and the supernatural appear to have been qualitatively different. The graves of the early human Skhul V and Jebel Qafzeh fossils contained *symbolic* tools—burial goods, the skull of a bear, and the horns of a deer grasped in their hands. Symbolic tools, a bishop's miter, a flag, and a holy image are qualitatively different from hammers, knives, saws, and computers. They provide clear signs of a *human* cognitive ability that can think about life and death and construct theories of life after death and the forces and spirits that rule the world and afterworld. Symbolic tools provide clear evidence of language that could convey these concepts.

Many Neanderthal fossils were deliberately buried, but evidence for symbolic tools is absent at Neanderthal burial sites until much later periods—for example, the cave bear skulls associated with the La Ferrassie Neanderthal burial site in France. However, specialists in the archaeology of Neanderthal culture, such as Paul Mellars of Cambridge University, believe that many of the stone tools, ornaments, and objects found in these late Neanderthal sites are borrowings from their anatomically modern human neighbors.[4] The flower pollen that Ralph Solecki found in the early Shanidar Neanderthal burial site was also scattered throughout the cave floor. The red ocher "pigment" that has been found in other Neanderthal graves may not have symbolized blood. It just as likely is the result of the natural decay of the untanned animal skins that they wore. Recent archaeological studies have applied new technology to this old question: Were Neanderthal hominids as intelligent as early modern human beings? The answer seems to be no; early modern humans appear to have devoted more thought to the problems of survival in an unforgiving world.

Daniel Lieberman of Rutgers University and John Shea of the State University of New York at Stony Brook analyzed the hunting techniques of early humans. They showed that humans living in the Levantine 30,000 years before the same region was occupied by Neanderthals used a hunting strategy different from that of Neanderthals. These early humans, presumably similar to the Skhul V and Jebel Qafzeh fossils, appeared to have followed the great herds of gazelles on which they fed, expending less effort because they had more opportunities to make a kill. In contrast, the Neanderthal populations that occupied these Middle Eastern regions 30,000 years later had a less efficient hunting strategy, expending more effort to obtain food. Lieberman and Shea obviously had no films or records of either Neanderthal or early human lifestyles. Their inferences are based on new technology, old teeth, and stone tools. Using a scanning electron microscope, Lieberman examined growth rings in the teeth of gazelles that had been hunted and eaten by early humans and Neanderthals. Teeth, like trees, have seasonal growth rings, though these are not visible to the eye or to conventional microscopes. The season of the year when these gazelles had been killed could be determined by an examination of the pattern of growth rings. Goats were raised at the Harvard University Experimental Farm under controlled conditions. The characteristics of growth rings of their teeth were different during the spring/summer and fall/winter seasons. Growth rings that are translucent under microscopic examination are laid down at a steady rate in the spring/summer season, between April and October; opaque growth rings are deposited at a slower rate during the fall/winter season, between November and March. Therefore, one can reliably ascertain the season in which an animal was killed by microscopically determining whether its teeth's growth rings are opaque or translucent.

Microscopic examination of the gazelle teeth in caves that were inhabited at different times by Neanderthals and by early modern humans, respectively, showed that the Neanderthals had brought gazelles back to the same cave home during both the spring/summer and the fall/winter seasons. Since gazelle herds migrate and are found in different locales in these seasons, the Neanderthal hunters must have traveled from this home base to hunt and return with their prey. In contrast, the tooth ring analysis showed that caves inhabited by early humans contained the remains of gazelles killed during one season. The most plausible conclusion is that early modern humans were nomadic and followed their gazelle prey through their seasonal migrations, a strategy that characterizes recent human hunter–gatherer societies. In contrast, the Neanderthals appear to have remained in a home base and to have traveled longer and longer distances to hunt the gazelle herds when they migrated away. Shea's analysis of their stone weapons is consistent with their hunting larger game at greater distances from their home base. They had to devote more time and effort to produce stone-tipped spears that would maximize their chances of hunting scarcer game. The more "advanced" Neanderthal stone spearpoints paradoxically may reflect *less* intelligent use of time and resources. More time and effort spent in hunting leaves less time for reflection and innovation.

Although the advances in tool technology that can be discerned in the archaeological record are often taken to be a sign of intellectual development, the lessons of history demonstrate the fallacy of directly equating material tools with brainpower. The weapons of the Roman legions were not significantly better than those of their adversaries. Tactics, which leave no trace in the archaeological record, were the key to Roman triumphs. In the forest paths of Germany the "barbarian" tribes triumphed when the Romans could not take advantage of their planned and rehearsed tactics, coordinated volleys of heavy spears, shield walls protecting advancing lines of troops, flanking maneuvers, envelopments—tactics still studied in war colleges. The different schema governing the use of the same "hunting tools" by Neanderthals and by early modern humans thus is significant. Their hunter-gatherer cultural patterns appear to have differed.

Nor can we link the pace of technological change to brainpower without taking the aggregations of culture into account. A simple example will suffice. The speed at which people can travel is one measure of technology. For millions of years 2 or 3 miles an hour was the limit set by humans' walking pace. About six thousand years ago horses were domesticated, and the maximum sustained rate jumped to about 15 miles an hour. That speed held constant until the early decades of the nineteenth century, when steam-powered locomotives were invented. Fifteen miles per hour was about the pace of the first steam-powered railroad trains, but within 70 years the maximum speed exceeded 100 miles an hour. By the 1940s military fighter planes flew at 200 miles an hour. Twenty-five years later commercial airliners routinely cruised at 540 miles an hour. Military aircraft now exceed 2,500 miles per hour and space shuttles and satellites circle the earth at 14,000 miles an hour. But are our brains different from those of the Indo-Europeans who first tamed horses six thousand years ago?

Talking

The roots of human language seem to reach back to the australopithecines who probably were making stone tools and who certainly were walking upright at least 4.1 million years ago. But does this mean that they had brains capable of language? That depends on what one thinks of as "language." Since chimpanzees can learn and acquire words, it would be implausible to suppose that the australopithecine brain was not capable of mastering this important component of human language. Merlin Donald, of Queen's University in Canada, one of the rare individuals capable of synthesizing data from disparate areas of science, presents a convincing argument for early hominid protolanguage, based on wordlike concepts that have a mimetic or imitative basis.

Donald's proposal is supported by the fact that deaf children raised without any exposure to formal sign language spontaneously develop, at about the age of three, gestural communication based on pantomime. The deaf children whom Susan Goldin-Meadow studied at the University of Chicago, for example, signaled "bottle opening" by forming an open bottleish shape with their left hand while "turning" an imaginary bottle lid with their right hand. Though australopithecine and *Homo habilis* brains might not have had this capacity at the age of three, they surely would have attained this level of mimetic ability by the age of five years, the age at which the Gardners' chimpanzees raised in human environments invented novel sign gestures.

Whether australopithecines or *Homo habilis* talked is another matter. Gordon Hewes, the University of Colorado linguist who first raised this interesting question in 1973, thinks that the earliest form of protolanguage used manual gestures, facial expressions (grins, lip protrusion, etc.), and posture—a sort of body language. Hewes reasoned that the earliest hominids, like present-day chimpanzees, could not talk and instead had to rely on manual gestures to communicate in protolanguage. But the evidence that points to a link between manual motor control and speech-producing ability wasn't known in 1973. As the next chapter elaborates, the brain mechanisms that control precise manual motor control in human beings are also implicated in speech production. The fossil record in 1973 also hadn't yet revealed early hominids like *Homo habilis* who clearly had *invented* stone tool technology, nor had it shown that some australopithecine hominids had fingers adapted for precise manual motor control.

Upright bipedal locomotion, the great initial hominid adaptation that differentiated the australopithecines from their ape cousins, set the stage for the evolution of human vocal language. It is supposed that bipedal upright locomotion was at first an adaptation to australopithecine life in the savannas of Plio-Pleistocene Africa five to two million years ago. Their hominid limbs could stand the stresses of upright locomotion as they roamed the open grasslands. However, upright posture also conferred another "preadaptive" advantage on australopithecines; it freed their hands. Upright bipedal locomotion is so much a part of human existence that we forget to consider how virtually every aspect of our existence would be affected if we *couldn't use our hands.* Speech communication can be regarded as a biological extension of upright posture's freeing hominid hands for work. We can make and use tools, push branches aside, move boulders, carry objects, and so on, while we talk. Mothers can carry helpless infants, We can keep our eyes on the path, a roaming child, the animal we are hunting, or the sunset we are admiring, while we talk.[5]

Reconstructing Fossil Vocal Tracts

The match between anatomy and behavior that allows us to infer that australopithecines actually walked (the changes in their bones would have been counterproductive if they had been strictly arbo-

real) also holds for the production of speech. The British comparative anatomist Victor Negus, whose career spanned the first half of
the twentieth century, for example, discovered that breathing efficiency is reduced in social animals that communicate with each
other vocally. Negus found that their larynges can more readily
produce complex melodies, but cannot open as widely when they
breathe, compared with the larynges of animals who vocalize less.

There is an anatomical trade-off. The vocal cords of the larynx,
which produce the melodic "intonation" of speech and animal
vocalizations (for example, the wailing of a cat or the howl of a
wolf), consist of a complex set of cartilages, muscles, and soft tissue.
The vocal cords must close to start the rapid opening-closing cycle
that produces "phonation," the almost periodic puffs of air that we
hear as the pitch of a person's voice or an animal's cry. In contrast,
they open wide to least obstruct the flow of air to the lungs during
breathing. Negus showed that the vocal cords of horses and animals
whose survival depends on running for long distances and breathing aerobically can open wide, so as to maintain an unobstructed air
path to their lungs. In contrast, the vocal cords of monkeys, apes,
and humans constrict the airway in order to enhance phonation.
Figure 4-3 shows how the human vocal cords never fully open
enough to allow air to flow unobstructed into the trachea, or windpipe. A horse's larynx, by contrast, can open to allow unobstructed
airflow. If hominid language really was conveyed entirely by means
of gestures over a period of millions of years, why would we have
retained the inefficient hominoid laryngeal air path constriction?

But, as we noted in the previous chapters, the activity of the
larynx itself is only one component of human speech. The key element is the changes in shape that the air passages above the larynx,
the supralaryngeal vocal tract, can make. If Neanderthals did not
have a modern human vocal tract, then what about australopithecines? When the skulls of australopithecines are compared with
those of present-day chimpanzees, it is evident that the areas of
their skull bases that relate to the vocal tract are virtually identical.
Figure 4-4 shows lateral (side) views of an adult chimpanzee and a
"gracile" australopithecine skull. A number of different australo-

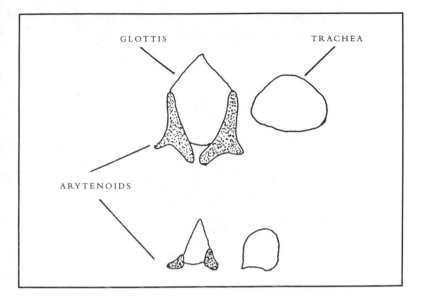

4-3—Airway Constriction of Horse versus Human Larynx
The upper-right sketch shows the cross-sectional area of the trachea (windpipe) of a horse. The sketch to the left shows the horse's vocal cords in their open, respiratory position. Note that the tracheal opening is not choked down.

The lower-right sketch shows the trachea of an adult human female. The tracing to the left shows her vocal cords in their open, respiratory position. Note that more than half of the tracheal opening is blocked. The problem arises because the human arytenoid cartilages (the stippled areas) are short. This allows better control of phonation, but interferes with respiration. All primates share the human condition in this respect and have larynges adapted for phonation at the expense of respiratory efficiency. (Adapted from Negus 1949)

pithecine species have been identified, but their skull bases do not materially differ in this respect. A visual inspection of any intact australopithecine skull base shows the long space between the basion, where the spinal column meets the skull, and the back of the hard palate. In chimpanzees and newborn human infants this space is where the high larynx is placed close to the opening to the nose. The distance between the basion and the front margin of the hard palate is also long, indicating a long mouth similar to that of a present-day chimpanzee. Edmund Crelin and I concluded in 1973 that australopithecine speech anatomy was not very different from that of chimpanzees (Lieberman 1975).

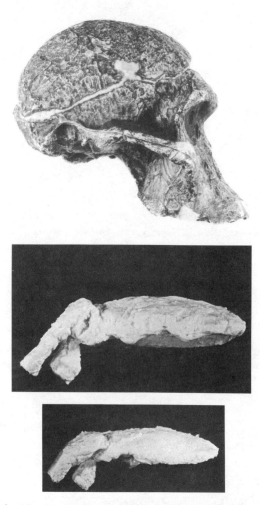

4-4—Australopithecine Skull and SVT and Chimpanzee SVT
Fossil *Australopithecus africanus* skull with reconstructed Supralaryngeal Vocal Tract (SVT) casting below it. The lower casting is a chimpanzee SVT. Both SVTs show the supralaryngeal airway in the position that would produce the vowel of the word *but*. (Adapted from Lieberman 1975)

Metrical analyses confirmed this reconstruction. Jeffrey Laitman, who completed his training in biological anthropology at Yale University with Edmund Crelin, teamed up with Ray Heimbuch, a statistician, to devise techniques that would allow them to compare the basicrania (skull bottoms) of living primates and then to correlate the skeletal measurements with the shape of their vocal tracts. Since human beings start with vocal tracts very similar to those of apes and monkeys and normally end up with adult vocal tracts, Laitman and Heimbuch included in their samples infants and children at various stages of development, as well as different species of monkeys and apes. Figure 4-5 shows the base of the skull of a chimpanzee with the skeletal measurements that Laitman made directly from the skulls.

The skeletal measurements that Laitman and Heimbuch used were taken directly from skulls, rather than from X-rays of living people and primates. Their estimates of the development of the human vocal tract also included measurements from cadavers. Their statistical analysis of skeletal measures roughly correlated with available development of the vocal tract in present-day human beings as they mature from birth to adulthood. In light of recent data that will be discussed below, their correlational technique cannot be regarded as an absolute index of vocal tract morphology in hominids. However, it provided a method that can take into account the variations that exist among the individuals who make up a species. Rhesus monkeys of all ages, for example, always had skeletal measurements similar to those of newborn human infants. Since newborn infants and rhesus monkeys have similar vocal tracts, this was to be expected. Having demonstrated that the statistical technique roughly correlated vocal tract morphology with skull measurements in human beings, Laitman and Heimbuch "plugged in" measurements made from fossil hominid skulls. To no one's surprise, their 1982 study showed that australopithecine skull measurements grouped with those of living monkeys, apes, and human infants, who do not have vocal tracts capable of producing the universal [i], [u], and [a] vowels of human languages. Australopithecines could probably lock their larynges into their noses, as present-day apes do. The australopithecine breathing airway was isolated from the food-liquid pathway during swallowing and the ingestion of small pieces of solid food. The single *Homo habilis* fossil skull that had sufficient remaining basicranial material (OH 24) appeared to have a somewhat more humanlike vocal tract, though it would still have been incapable of producing the full range of human speech sounds.[6]

An earlier study by Laitman and Heimbuch, published in 1979, applied the same statistical techniques to measurements of the skull bases of three of the classic Neanderthal fossils of those inhabiting Europe until 35,000 years ago: the adult La Chapelle-aux-Saints and La Ferrassie I fossils from France and the Gibraltar I Neanderthal in that English bastion at the tip of Spain. The analysis also considered the Teshik-Tash Neanderthal child, the Broken Hill African fossil, and the Cro-Magnon fossil who is sometimes equated with modern humans. The statistical procedure placed most of the European Neanderthal fossils close to the inferred modern human developmental ape group with the adult La Chapelle-aux-Saints fossil, somewhat between a two-year-old human child and the ape group. However, there were puzzling variations; some adult Neanderthal skulls seemed more or less modern than others. At about the same time as the Laitman and Heimbuch analyses, Clotilde Grosmangin in Paris made independent comparisons of the skull bases of the La Chapelle-aux-Saints and La Ferrassie I adult male Neanderthal skulls from the original fossil remains at the Musée de l'Homme in Paris with a broad sample of human and ape skulls. The modern human Cro-Magnon fossil was also measured, as well as one Neanderthal child (the Pech de l'Azé, estimated age two years). Grosmangin, like Edmund Crelin, on the basis of her direct visual comparison grouped the Neanderthal skulls with those of chimpanzees and human newborn infants. However, new data call for a reappraisal of the conclusions of these studies, including the 1971 Lieberman and Crelin study. The Neanderthal vocal tract most likely did not retain the primitive ape-human newborn morphology. Nonetheless, these new data still indicate that Neanderthals probably did not have speech capabilities equivalent to those of modern human beings.

This reappraisal rests on a new analysis by Robert McCarthy and Daniel Lieberman at Rutgers University (in press) based on a series of X-rays of infants and children and chimpanzees. McCarthy and Lieberman followed the development of the soft tissue of the vocal tract and the bony structure of the skull from the age of three months to the age of eighteen years. They found that the flexion of the skull base, one of the principal metrics used in previous studies to predict the shape of the vocal tract, does not have a clear relation to the vocal tract. The unflexed skull base of a chimpanzee is apparent in the shallow angle formed by the bones near the basion in Figure 4-4. Human adults, in contrast, have a flexed skull base; they also have a flexed vocal tract, in which the mouth and pharynx form an almost 90-degree angle and are equally long. However, McCarthy and Lieberman's metrical analysis shows that the change in flexion in humans is unrelated to the changes in the vocal tract that occur after birth. The change in skull base flexion occurs before the vocal tract reaches its adult proportions, between the ages of six to seven years. The pattern of growth that determines the angulation of the skull base, moreover, is different in chimpanzees and human beings. In other words, though valid statistical techniques differentiate the flexed adult human skull base from those of newborn humans and chimpanzees, the angulation of the skull base cannot be used to infer the shape of a fossil hominid's vocal tract. It has already changed from an unflexed to a flexed shape *before* the adultlike human vocal tract develops.

These new studies also clear up some hitherto vexing questions. Studies of the development of speech in human children (Lieberman 1980) show that some six-year-old children produce sounds such as the vowels [i] and [u] with formant frequency patterns equivalent to those of adults. This was puzzling since earlier studies of vocal tract development that had been based on a limited number of cadavers of children seemed to show that vocal tract development was not complete at this age. So how could children produce these sounds? The answer is that vocal tract measurements based on the distorted soft tissue of a cadaver are misleading. The vocal tracts of normal six- to seven-year-old children have already attained the human configuration in which the oral cavity and pharynx have equal lengths. One further question that immediately arises is how children can say words such as *see* (which in phonetic notation is [si]) at the age of two years, when their vocal tracts have not yet attained the adult human shape? The answer, in this case, is that they really are not producing well-formed [i]s. Acoustic analysis bears this out (Buhr 1980; Lieberman 1980). We "hear" their attempts as [i]s because of a perceptual "magnetic effect" that was discovered by Patricia Kuhl at the University of Washington in Seattle. Kuhl and an international team of speech scientists (including Kenneth Stevens at MIT and Bjorn Lindblom at the University of Stockholm) found that humans hear vowel formant frequencies that are close to the true values of an [i] as perfect [i]s (Kuhl et al. 1992). Exposure early in life to different languages results in different perceptual "magnets" that, in effect, pull in deviant formant frequency patterns toward a prototypical pattern. Infants exposed tò Swedish differ in this respect from infants exposed to English; they show slightly different magnet effects that correspond to the different vowel systems of Swedish and English. One moral of Kuhl's research is that perceptual judgments based on unaided ears cannot be substituted for acoustical analyses.

Returning to the Neanderthal question, the new McCarthy and Lieberman study based on undistorted X-ray images of living human subjects and chimpanzees reaffirms that Neanderthals (and archaic fossil hominids such as the various australopithecine species) did *not* have vocal tracts that could produce the full range of human speech. The long mouths of archaic hominids, including Neanderthals, made it improbable for them to have vocal tracts with an equally long pharynx. A long pharynx would have placed their larynges in their chests—a most improbable position (Lieberman 1984). The length of a fossil hominid's mouth can be determined with certainty from a reasonably intact skull base by measuring the distance between the incisors and the basion, which marks the point of the spinal column. As was noted earlier, the long Neanderthal mouth precludes its having a vocal tract in which the pharynx and mouth have about the same length.

The sketch in Figure 4-5 shows why a classic Neanderthal hominid could not have had a human vocal tract. The human tongue is almost circular in a side view. The upper part of the tongue, which forms the lower part of our mouth, is as long as the vertical back part, which forms the anterior (front-facing) part of

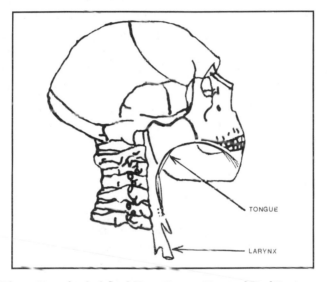

4-5—Why a Neanderthal Could Not Have a Human Vocal Tract
If we place a modern human tongue that corresponds to a mouth and pharynx that have equal lengths on the "classic" La Chapelle-aux-Saints fossil, the larynx ends up positioned *below* the neck. That's most unlikely. The tongue contour for this sketch was derived from cineradiographic studies of living humans talking by Peter Ladefoged and his colleagues at UCLA; it is the tongue of a normal adult woman. A smaller tongue would not be able to push food backward and downward to enable the Neanderthal to swallow. The spinal column of the Neanderthal is modern and has the lordosis, or curvature, of a normal human adult. The skull is also positioned on the standard "Frankfurt" plane used to compare the skulls of various primates. The problem arises because the length of the Neanderthal mouth is outside the range of modern human beings. William Howells at Harvard University established this fact by studying different human population groups.

the pharynx. The primary function of the tongue is to ingest food; it must be able to propel food toward the back of the mouth and then downward. This means that the tongue normally almost fills the mouth.[7] In this illustration a modern human female tongue has been scaled to "fit" the mouth of the La Chapelle-aux-Saints Neanderthal fossil. The Neanderthal fossil has been given a modern vertebral column and is oriented on the standard "Frankfurt" plane used to compare the skulls of different primates. Because the Neanderthal mouth is long, the pharynx must also be long *if* we insist that the Neanderthal was capable of producing fully modern human speech. However, the long pharynx places the larynx very, very low—in the creature's chest. Since no primate has its larynx positioned in its chest, we've created a very improbable monster. The situation would be worse if we had placed a male human tongue in the male Neanderthal skull; human males tend to have slightly longer pharynges.[8]

The detailed reassessment of Neanderthal speech capabilities is still in progress. The precise proportions of the Neanderthal vocal tract will not be evident until the comparative study of fossil remains and human development directed by Daniel Lieberman is completed.[9] However, it is clear that the Neanderthal vocal tract was not, as Edmund Crelin and I thought in 1971, exactly like a human newborn's. Preliminary data indicate that the vocal tract of a classic Neanderthal fossil like La Chapelle-aux-Saints probably had the capabilities of at least a two-year-old human child; it would not have been able to produce the full range of human speech sounds, particularly not the vowels [i] and [u], which with [a] optimize the acoustic "distinctiveness" of human speech. This would be true even if we placed the Neanderthal larynx in the same position that it has in a normal adult human relative to the vertebral column and lower jaw. The Neanderthal mouth is still much longer than the pharynx.[10] Fortunately, the Neanderthal vocal tract reconstruction that we computer modeled in 1971 allowed for this contingency; Edmund Crelin presciently placed the reconstructed Neanderthal larynx lower than a human newborn's to allow for the uncertainties of reconstruction. In short, Neanderthal speech anatomy was more advanced than that of *Homo erectus* or human newborns but still incapable of producing the full range of human speech sounds with the stability and formant frequency structure of sounds like the "supervowel" [i]. Neanderthal speech probably was nasalized.

In short, the retention by Neanderthals of the primitive prognathous face typical of earlier hominids, in which the lower face is positioned in front of the brain, clearly indicates less efficient speech communication. They represent an intermediate stage in the evolution of human speech. Although their brain was as large as our own, the neural substrate that regulates speech production may also have been less developed. The studies discussed in the next chapter link the neuroanatomical structures implicated in speech production to other aspects of language and cognition, which also may have been less developed in Neanderthals. However, it is impossible to categorically state that the linguistic and cognitive ability of Neanderthals actually was less developed than that of our immediate ancestors.

In contrast, the fossil specimens of early modern human beings—Skhul V, Jebel Qafzeh, and Afalou—clearly had skulls that could not have supported a high larynx position; they must instead have had human vocal tracts. The distinctive qualities of human speech production derive from the almost equal lengths of the mouth and the pharynx. The equal length of these air passages allows us to produce the formant patterns of vowels such as [i] with relatively imprecise articulatory gestures. The elegant computer modeling study of René Carré of the CNRS in Paris, Bjorn Lindblom of Stockholm University, and Peter MacNeilage of the University of Texas at Austin replicates Kenneth Stevens's 1972 study, which first explicitly pointed out this fact. It is impossible to generate the formant frequency patterns of the vowels [i] and [u] without having a vocal tract in which the tongue can move to form abrupt changes in the diameter of the pharynx and oral cavities.[11] The study by Carré, Lindblom, and MacNeilage indeed shows that a computer model of a nonhuman primate vocal tract programmed to optimize the acoustic distinctiveness of speech will "grow" a pharynx and achieve the modern human configuration. In other words, modern human speech is inherently "clearer," easier to understand, because we have a vocal tract in which the mouth and pharynx have roughly equal lengths.

Speech and the Mating Game

Evolutionary biologists may disagree on whether the pace of evolution is always gradual or whether sudden changes occur. However, they all accept the proposition that "genetic isolation," which prevents different populations of a species from mating, is one of the primary mechanisms for the creation of a new species. If two groups never mate, their genes are likely to diverge. Ethologists have noted that songbirds literally sing for their partners. Birdsongs serve as "genetic isolating mechanisms." Frogs also find their mates by their less melodic croaks.

Recent genetic studies show that human beings, too, tend to mate and have children with partners who talk as they do. Guido Barbujani and Robert Sokal, geneticists at the State University of New York at Stony Brook, investigated the patterns of genetic variation in present-day Europe. They found that sharp genetic "boundaries" (measured in genetic factors that are "neutral," conferring no selective advantages, such as resistance to malaria) occur where they might be expected—for example, along the high mountains of the Alps or the watery expanses that physically keep potential brides and grooms apart. However, other sharp genetic boundaries arose in the absence of any physical obstacles. South and north German dialects, for instance, produce as sharp a genetic distinction as the alpine mountain barriers of the Matterhorn and Monte Rosa. Similar effects occur along the Po River in adjacent towns where different dialects of Italian have been spoken for a thousand years. In short, stable, long-term relations that produce progeny—that is, marriages—tend to happen between people who speak the same dialect.

These effects would have been magnified in the prehistoric era in which both modern human beings and Neanderthals inhabited the world. Modern human beings can as children effortlessly acquire the dialect of any human language with "native" proficiency before the age of seven years or so, usually with only slight traces of an "accent" before puberty. But Neanderthals were inherently unable to produce human speech—they would have sounded like a village idiot incapable of talking "right." Perhaps the folk concept of village idiot speech reflects that distant past when Neanderthals and modern human populations populated Eurasia. If our ancestors behaved as we do, which is the most reasonable premise, then Neanderthal speech would have yielded a genetic isolating mechanism that would have kept early human and Neanderthal populations apart even if they lived in physical and temporal proximity. Therefore, we can account for the fact that Neanderthal and early modern human populations coexisted for tens of thousands of years. The demographic model developed by Ezra Zubrow, of the State University of New York at Buffalo, shows that Neanderthals would gradually have become extinct over many generations if (a) their early modern human competitors possessed only slight advantages and (b) they were genetically isolated. We have only to establish slight differences, such as those that may have existed in the way that Neanderthals and early humans hunted. Over the course of time even a slight advantage in coping with nature would have led to the increase of our human ancestors and a struggle for available resources. That is the pattern commonly observed for species competing in the same ecological niche. Again, given the isolating effects of dialect, a small difference in linguistic and/or cognitive ability, operating over many generations, could have resulted in Neanderthal extinction. Thus, the sounds of speech in themselves can account for the extinction of the Neanderthals.

CHAPTER 5

Talking and
Thinking Brains

IT WOULD BE PRESUMPTUOUS to state that science understands how the human brain works. Every new discovery raises new questions, but it is safe to state that the last twenty years have seen remarkable advances in our understanding of some of the principles that govern the physiology and the evolution of biological brains. These new insights suggest that the parts of the brain that regulate the production of human speech are also implicated in the neural processes by which we pull words out of the brain's dictionary, interpret their meaning, determine the syntax of a sentence, and finally comprehend meaning. The neural bases of human speech motor control and syntax appear to be part of a unique human "functional language system" that evolved to produce and comprehend spoken language. Moreover, many of the neuroanatomical structures that process speech and written language are also implicated in other aspects of cognition. Therefore, the first early modern humans who had brains that could regulate the complex articulatory maneuvers necessary for speech would most likely have possessed fully human cognitive-linguistic capacities as well.

Biological Brains and Digital Computers

The architecture of the human brain clearly is not the biological equivalent of a conventional digital computer. Every age constructs a model of the brain that reflects the most complex technology of the day. In the 1920s brains were often compared to telephone exchanges. The prevailing model of the human brain until recently has been the digital computer.

The design of a conventional digital computer is "modular." Discrete devices accomplish particular tasks. We can purchase a new module and with suitable connecting cables and software add new capacities to a computer's repertoire. If, for example, we want to join the Internet, we can add a telephone modem and software to an existing computer. All we need is the necessary cash or credit. Digital computers have changed the way we live and work; they are *the* emblems of modern technology. It is therefore not surprising that the brain model presented in virtually all current discussions of language or human evolution is derived from the architecture of conventional digital computers. Moreover, for the past thirty years the linguistic study of language has been dominated by Noam Chomsky at MIT. Superb neurophysiologists who understand that brains are *not* the biological equivalents of digital computers work at MIT. However, Chomsky's model of the brain still seems to be based on the digital computers that were being developed at MIT when he first developed his linguistic theories in the mid-1950s. The technologies that now allow clinicians to image the brains of patients suffering brain damage that destroys their capacity to understand and produce language did not exist at that time. The state of knowledge concerning the human brain had hardly changed since the nineteenth century, and so it was reasonable for Chomsky to propose that the human brain contained an additional "organ," a language "module" that wasn't present in the brains of closely related animals such as chimpanzees. Chomsky's model, moreover, was a reasonable interpretation of the traditional textbook treatment of the human brain, which attributes language to two parts of the brain—Broca's and Wernicke's areas, named after the nineteenth-century scientists who were among the first clinicians to study the effects of brain damage on language. However, though these parts of the brain are involved in language, the data of hundreds of independent research projects using new techniques show that there is much more to the story.

Aphasia

The classical account of the human brain's capacity for language is based on nineteenth-century studies of the effects of strokes that destroy parts of the brain. Paul Broca in 1861 described the speech production deficits that occurred after massive damage to the frontal regions of the left hemisphere of the brain of one of his patients. The left hemisphere controls many aspects of motor control of the right arm and leg, and Broca's patient also had severe motor control impairment. Postmortem examination of the patient's brain revealed that part of the neocortex, the outermost region of the patient's brain, had been destroyed, as had subcortical brain structures.

A useful way of visualizing both the structure and the evolutionary history of the brain is to think of it as a three-layered onion. The innermost parts are found in animals whose skeletal structures are similar to very ancient vertebrates. The middle layer of the brain evolved in later animals that resemble present-day reptiles. The outer layers of the brain evolved most recently in mammals, the outer "neocortex" being most developed in primates and human beings.[1] Human beings, in particular, have a vastly enlarged neocortex compared with even that of our most closely related cousins, chimpanzees. Since speech is a capacity that exists only in humans, Broca probably reasoned that his patient's speech production deficits must have derived from the damage to the neocortex, the most recent "phylogenetic" (evolutionary) addition to the brain. Broca's region is sketched in Figure 5-1, together with Wernicke's area, a posterior (back) part of the neocortex that Karl Wernicke, a nineteenth-century German neurologist who also studied the effects of brain damage, claimed regulated the comprehension of spoken language.

Subsequent studies of Broca's aphasia established some general patterns. Speech production is labored and impaired; patients have difficulty regulating the sequencing of the muscles that control speech production. Manual motor control is also impaired. However, the language deficits of Broca's aphasia transcend motor control. Broca's aphasia can yield "anomia," which renders patients unable to name objects or pictures of objects or actions. Both the production and the comprehension of distinctions in meaning conveyed by syntax is disrupted. English-speaking patients often utter sentences in which they omit articles and prepositions, words that convey grammatical distinctions. Similar effects occur in patients who speak other languages. Broca's aphasia is sometimes equated with

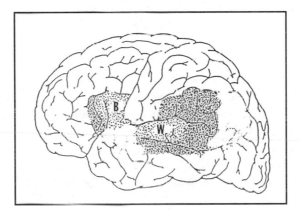

5-1—Broca's and Wernicke's Areas
Lateral view of the surface of the left side of a human brain showing the traditional "sites" of language, Broca's area (B) and Wernicke's area (W). The theory represented in this diagram, though traditional, is obsolete. The neural bases of human language involve many other neocortical areas, which can be pictured in diagrams of the surface of the brain, and subcortical neuroanatomical structures. Circuits connecting various neuroanatomical structures are implicated in many aspects of human language.

"expressive" difficulties, although it is clear that the deficits are not limited to expressive language, since the comprehension of distinctions in meaning conveyed by syntax also can be impaired. Patients can have difficulty comprehending sentences with moderately complex syntax. They might not know, for example, who is being chased in the sentence "The girl was being chased by the boy." The brain damage that has traditionally been linked to Wernicke's aphasia is in a posterior region of the brain associated with the perception of sounds and vision. Wernicke's aphasia is sometimes equated with perceptual deficits. Patients are unable to understand the meanings of words; they utter sounds that sound like words but are actually non-words, producing fluent but meaningless speech. If it were actually true that damage localized to these regions of the human brain caused these exclusively linguistic deficits, then we might have isolated the "seats" of language.

However, this is not the case. Broca was in fact operating within the framework of "phrenology," a theory that claimed that particular parts of the neocortex regulated various aspects of human behavior. Phrenologists tried to relate bumps on the skull to very specific aspects of behavior, such as avarice, honesty, or mathematical ability. Phrenology has been dismissed as quack science— bumps on the skull do not correspond to expected behavior—but its essence survived in Broca's work and, more recently, in Chomskian "modular" brain theory. The patient whom Broca studied did sustain damage to the neocortical area named for Broca. However, he had also suffered extensive damage to the subcortical areas, beneath the neocortex. Although other neurologists challenged Broca's localization of language in the brain, his views prevailed until it became possible to see the actual pattern of brain damage in living patients.[2]

New techniques introduced in the 1970s and 1980s, computerized tomography (CT) and magnetic resonance imaging (MRI), allow neurologists to view the inside of a living person's brain. Both techniques involve computer processing of X-ray imaging (CT scans) and signals induced by magnetic fields (MRI), respectively; they yield images of "slices" of the brain from which damage can be assessed. It has become clear that most complex aspects of human behavior, including language, are not regulated in a single localized region of the brain. The difference between a biological brain and a conventional digital computer is that although discrete neuroanatomical structures can be identified in the human brain, they regulate different aspects of behavior by means of "circuits" formed of "neurons" (the basic computational units of brains) within each structure that connect to neurons in different neuroanatomical structures. Damage anywhere along a circuit can result in a specific behavioral deficit. Massive brain damage to a neuroanatomical structure that is involved in many circuits can disrupt different aspects of behavior.

Functional Neural Circuits

Circuit models like those developed by Jeffrey Cummings of the UCLA School of Medicine, M-Marsel Mesulam of the Harvard Neurology Department, and Hannah and Antonio Damasio of the University of Iowa School of Medicine are now accepted as possible models of the functional anatomy of the human brain. It has become clear that the comprehension of a sentence involves circuits that link many cortical and subcortical neural structures (the inner layers of the onion) distributed throughout the brain. Standard medical texts, written by eminent neurosurgeons and neurologists, such as Donald Stuss and D. Frank Benson's *The Frontal Lobes*, note that permanent "big Broca's" aphasia occurs only when subcortical damage disrupts the language circuits. As Stuss and Benson observe, patients who have brain damage limited to the traditional neocortical "sites" of language, Broca's and Wernicke's areas, generally recover after a few months. A study at Brown University that my colleagues and I have just completed dramatically demonstrates this point. We studied the linguistic and cognitive behavior of a person who had suffered severe cortical damage that completely destroyed Wernicke's area without any apparent subcortical damage. We fortunately had hours of tape recordings that the subject had made before his stroke when he presented formal papers and responded to questions at conferences. Acoustic and linguistic analysis showed absolutely no differences between his speech, syntax, or vocabulary before and after the stroke. Nor did a full battery of linguistic and psychological tests reveal any signs or symptoms of Wernicke's aphasia. Yet highly qualified specialists who read the MRI images of his brain agree that the cortical damage to his brain includes Wernicke's area. The subject clearly did not relearn language; he retained his original regional dialect.

These new findings demonstrate that the function of the traditional cortical sites of language, Broca's and Wernicke's areas, is unclear. However, new techniques such as positron emission tomography (PET) and functional magnetic resonance imaging (FMRI) may help us solve the mystery. These techniques allow us to determine what parts of the human brain are most active when we perform different tasks. They essentially monitor metabolic activity—as is the case for muscles, parts of the brain that work harder consume more energy. The activity of normal, intact brains can be monitored as well as that of brains of persons suffering from neurodegenerative diseases and lesions that affect various parts of their brains.

PET studies, moreover, show that the prefrontal regions of the brain long associated with "non-linguistic" cognition are implicated in language. The prefrontal regions of victims of Broca's aphasia are not as active as those of normal persons; similar effects occur in Parkinson's disease, which affects subcortical basal ganglia circuits that transmit information to and from prefrontal cortex.[3] Prefrontal cortex is implicated in various aspects of higher cognition in human beings, such as problem solving, deriving the "abstract" principles that underlie specific problems, or changing strategies when that is appropriate.[4] These PET studies are consistent with traditional clinical observations and formal tests showing that Broca's aphasia does not produce "purely" linguistic deficits. Kurt Goldstein, one of the most distinguished aphasiologists of the middle decades of the twentieth century, pointed out that Broca's aphasia resulted in a loss of what he termed "the abstract capacity." A patient might be able to perform routine tasks and engage in polite, though meaningless, conversation but would be unable to plan ahead or solve problems that involved more than rote responses to simple familiar questions. In one extreme case, a patient would automatically switch on the light when he entered a darkened room, but be unable to switch the lights on when he was asked to do that.

In short, the pattern of deficits associated with Broca's aphasia—loss of manual and speech motor control, syntax comprehension and abstract cognition, and anomia—appears to derive from damage to *neural circuits*. The basic computing elements of the brain that constitute these circuits are neurons, cells that, when activated, produce an electrical signal that is transmitted to other neurons. The signal transmitted from an activated neuron travels outward through its "axon," a biological equivalent of the wires that transmit electrical signals from one computer chip to another in the electrical pathways or circuits that connect the computing and memory devices of a computer. However, neuronal circuits differ from conventional computer circuits in many ways. Each neuron can receive "input" information from "dendrites" that connect to the neurons through "synapses." Dendrites can be thought of as wires that transmit electrical signals. Synapses can be thought of as a biological analog of a volume control of a radio. Turning the volume control up or down passes more or less of the electrical signal to the radio's amplifier, resulting in a louder or quieter sound. An analogous process occurs neurally; modification of a synapse can lead the signal transmitted by a dendrite to have a greater or lesser effect on neuronal activity. By these means, signals from the dendrites that constitute the total input to a neuron can "trigger" it to transmit a signal to other neurons.[5]

Microscopic examination of the structure of the brain and techniques that use special chemical compounds that "trace" out the complex circuitry of the brain show that groups of neurons (or "populations") in one area of the cortex connect (or "project") to groups of neurons in another region of the cortex or to some particular subcortical structure. These populations of neurons, in turn,

project to other groups of neurons forming independent ("segregated") circuits. A particular neuroanatomical structure, for example, the substantia nigra, a structure deep within the brain, has
many different independent circuits that connect with different
neuroanatomical structures.

Tracer techniques cannot be used on human beings. The tracer chemicals (some techniques use viruses) must be injected into
the brain or nerves of a living animal. The animal is then sacrificed
and its brain stained with dyes that attach themselves to the tracer
agent. The brain is then sectioned into extremely thin slices, in
which the colored dye trace can be viewed under a microscope.
Tracer studies of the brains of monkeys have shown that neural
circuits link various areas of the neocortex to the prefrontal cortex
through subcortical brain structures such as the basal ganglia.[6] The
structures of the basal ganglia, such as the putamen, caudate nucleus, and globus pallidus (the names are fanciful descriptive Latin
terms that anatomists gave to these structures hundreds of years
ago), exist in reptiles as well as in mammals. However, they took on
new functions during the course of evolution. Reptiles lack a neocortex; their basal ganglia constitute the "highest" level of their
brains in which sensory information is evaluated to initiate appropriate motor activity. In mammals, which possess cortical brain
mechanisms, basal ganglia also process sensory information and
regulate motor activity, but they have taken on new functions. In
mammals basal ganglia also serve to channel information between
various areas of the neocortex. Many neurological disturbances in
humans (such as Parkinson's and Huntington's diseases, obsessive-
compulsive behavior, depression) can be traced to disrupted basal
ganglia circuits. The diagrams in Figure 5-2 show some of the
hypothetical neural circuits that may be implicated in different
behavioral deficits, ranging from the flouting of social conventions
to profound motor and cognitive disturbances.

Clinical neurologists like Jeffrey Cummings have found that
damage or reduced activity in any of the neuroanatomical structures involved in a neural circuit can result in a similar behavioral
problem. Neurodegenerative diseases such as Parkinson's, which is

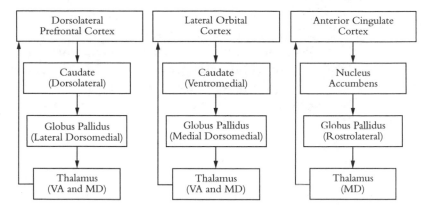

5-2—Some Probable Neural Circuits Regulating Various Behaviors
Some of the circuits connecting populations of neurons in frontal neocortical areas, anterior cingulate cortex (motor cortex), and different parts of subcortical neuroanatomical structures (caudate, globus pallidus, nucleus accumbens, and thalamus). The symbols VA and MD indicate ventral anterior and medial dorsal parts of the thalamus. The schematized circuits (various indirect circuits involving substantia nigra are omitted) are based on clinical studies of human patients; they are being continually revised as new data become available. The circuits regulate different aspects of behavior. The dorsolateral prefrontal circuit, for example, is implicated in cognitive behavior and language; the anterior cingulate circuit, in emotional disturbances; etc. Localized brain damage that destroys any part of a circuit yields similar symptoms. Major damage that destroys a neuroanatomical structure will result in a wide range of behavioral deficits. (After Cummings 1993)

caused by a reduction in the level of dopamine, a "neurotransmitter" necessary for normal basal ganglia function, can result in both cognitive and motor deficits. Cummings and virtually all neurologists now believe that these behavioral deficits occur because human basal ganglia structures are implicated in the neural circuits regulating these different activities. The neural circuit details are based on tracer and microelectrode studies of monkeys and other animals, in which exceedingly fine electrodes, placed in the brain of an animal, record the electrical activity within a neuron or the activity of nearby neurons. Direct data on human brains are not available, but the circuits are probably similar in human beings.

Two levels of brain architecture, therefore, must be kept in mind. Particular, discrete neuroanatomical structures appear to perform specific operations, such as sequencing patterns of brain activity. However, a particular neuroanatomical structure can perform this operation in many independent neural circuits that connect different neuroanatomical structures in complex distributed networks. Circuits seem to be the neural "elements" that regulate an observable aspect of behavior, such as picking up a pencil from a table. Though this seems superficially to be a simple act, it involves a complex set of neural computations integrating visual information, tactile information, and motor activity with the position of your arms, hand, body, and so on with respect to the pencil. In other words, complex aspects of human and animal behavior involve the activity of many different parts of the brain connected together in "functional neural circuits."[7] The tracer and electrode techniques that neurophysiologists usually use to study functional neural circuits obviously cannot be used in human subjects. Therefore, since only human beings possess language, it is not possible to get direct evidence on the functional neural circuits that might regulate various aspects of language, but we can see how functional neural systems are organized by studying aspects of behavior common to humans and closely related animals like monkeys. Manual motor control keyed to visual cues is an obvious choice since the evolution of enhanced vision and manual motor control played an important part in shaping the primate brain. Functional neural systems appear to have evolved to achieve particular behaviors that enhance an animal's survival and the survival of progeny. One system, explored by Charles Gross and his colleagues at Princeton University, appears to be adapted to grasping or deflecting objects that are moving toward a monkey's face. Their studies, which were published in 1995, of the macaque monkey (*Macaca fasicularis*) brain show that cells in the putamen, a subcortical basal ganglia structure, respond vigorously when small objects approach the monkey's face and eyes. These brain cells (putamenal neurons) do not respond to stationary objects or to moving objects more than a meter or so from the monkey; they respond only when objects move close. About 25 percent of these sites also respond to tactile sensations on the monkey's face. These sites in the putamen, in turn, communicate to neurons in the monkey's premotor neocortex, which, in turn, activate the monkey's arms. This functional close-object-intercept system links inputs from visual cortex, tactile receptors, putamen, premotor cortex, motor cortex, and the monkey's arms and hands, integrating sight, touch, and muscular control to achieve a specific task—intercepting objects. The point, which can scarcely be overemphasized, is that the neural hardware that constitutes this functional neural system is not located in one particular "box" in the brain.

Some confusion, unfortunately, can arise if you go beyond this discussion and read linguistic studies that use the term *module* in a very different manner. Neurophysiologists often use *module* to characterize a functional neural circuit that carries out a particular task. It is clear that our brains contain hundreds, if not thousands, of neural circuits. The studies that will be reviewed in this chapter also show that although some aspects of neural circuitry are specified by our genes, the detailed circuits that carry out various motor tasks, interpret the visual world, and code our knowledge of the world are acquired as we experience life. In contrast, linguists and philosophers often use the term *module* to refer to a genetically specified part of the brain that carries out some specific aspect of behavior, such as coding the rules of grammar.[8]

Research on Parkinson's Disease

Parkinson's disease has become one of the most intensively studied "experiment in nature" because it reveals the role of circuits involving subcortical basal ganglia structures in regulating human speech, language, and thinking. The cause of the disease, which usually strikes people in their sixties, is unknown. The primary symptoms involve motor control, tremors, impaired walking, rigid muscles, and slow movements. But Parkinson's can also result in cognitive losses—the problems being similar to the loss of the "abstract capacity" noted by Kurt Goldstein for Broca's aphasia. My colleagues and I found that a primary speech motor deficit of Broca's aphasia also occurs in Parkinson's. Moreover, Parkinson's patients can have deficits in the comprehension of syntax similar to those of Broca's aphasia.

Acoustic analyses of the speech production deficits of many Parkinson's patients show that they are unable to clearly articulate "stop consonants" (such as the English consonants [b], [p], [d], [t], [g], and [k]). Their attempts to say *pat* result in *bat*, *dad* becomes *tad*, *god* becomes *cod*, and so forth. When you produce these sounds, you must first open the closed supralaryngeal airway by rapidly opening your lips for a [b] or a [p], or lowering your tongue for the other stop consonants. This articulatory maneuver results in a sudden "burst" of sound. You then must precisely adjust the vocal cords of your larynx so that phonation starts no more than 20/1000 of a second (20 msec) after the burst for the "voiced" [b], [d], or [g]. Phonation must start at an interval longer than 20 msec for the "unvoiced" [p], [t], and [k]. The primary acoustic difference between the words *bat* and *pat*, for example, derives from the precise control of this short interval of time. Phonation must occur within 20 msec after the burst for *bat*; the time delay between the burst and phonation must exceed 20 msec when you instead say *pat*. Many Parkinson's disease patients are unable to regulate this timing, which speech scientists term voice onset time (VOT).

In other words, VOT is simply the time that intervenes between the burst of sound and the onset of periodic phonation produced by the larynx. Linguists have observed that similar VOT distinctions differentiate stop consonants in all human languages. In the early nineteenth century the German physiologist Johannes Müller, one of the founders of modern psychology and physiology, observed that these consonants were also among the first ones that children learned to say. They are among the few attested "universals" of human language.[9] This minimal time difference corresponds to a constraint of our auditory system, which does not differ in this respect from that of most mammals. It becomes very difficult to tell which of two different sounds came first when the interval of time between them is shorter than 20 msec. Similar effects on VOT were noted for Mandarin Chinese–speaking Parkinson's patients who were studied by Dr. Chu-Yu Tseng and myself in a project at the Academia Sinica in Taiwan.

Sheila Blumstein and her colleagues at the Boston Veterans Administration Hospital, where aphasia has been intensively studied for many years, first noted this speech-timing problem for Broca's aphasics in a study published in 1980. Broca's aphasics are unable to maintain control of the sequencing between their lips and tongue maneuvers and laryngeal control; their intended [b]s may be heard as [p]s, [t]s as [d]s, and so on. Independent studies have since shown that this is one of the primary speech motor deficits of Broca's aphasics and many Parkinson's patients.[10] We can trace the problem in Parkinson's disease to impaired basal ganglia function; the VOTs of many of the Chinese-speaking patients whom Chu-Yu Tseng and I studied became more distinct when they were treated with L-dopa, a drug that increases dopamine levels, restoring basal ganglia function temporarily.[11]

Deficits in the comprehension of distinctions in meaning conveyed by syntax and in abstract reasoning similar to those of Broca's aphasics can also occur in Parkinson's disease. We can be almost certain that these impairments reflect the deterioration of basal ganglia circuits that connect prefrontal cortex to other parts of the brain. Trevor Robbin's research group at Cambridge University showed by means of elegant computer-administered cognitive tests that the scores and response times of Parkinson's patients dramatically improved when they received L-dopa.[12] Chu-Yu Tseng and I have noted similar effects for the comprehension of Chinese syntax. The syntax comprehension problems resembled those that my colleague Joseph Friedman, the director of several large-scale Parkinson's disease studies, and I first reported in 1990. We studied English-speaking Parkinson's patients. Similar problems in comprehending sentences in which you have to keep track of distinctions conveyed by syntax, rather than real-world knowledge, have been noted for native speakers of Greek and for English speakers by several research groups working independently.[13]

Atop Mount Everest

As you ascend a mountain, the pressure and oxygen content of the air decrease. Mild to severe reactions to the lack of oxygen, or "hypoxia," can occur. Most people can adjust to the lower oxygen content of mountains if they ascend slowly, but a few can have difficulties even at relatively low elevations. The immediate effects of "acute mountain sickness" include headaches, vomiting, and disorientation. Motor coordination can become seriously impaired; indeed, one simple test for acute stages of mountain sickness is to see whether a person can walk in a straight line. Descent to lower altitudes is imperative for those suffering acute mountain sickness.

On one climb in Switzerland on the Matterhorn I saw a strong, young athlete collapse at 4,000 meters. He had flown directly from Seattle, Washington, where he lived most of the year at sea level, and had started the Matterhorn climb the day after he arrived in Switzerland. An Air Zermatt helicopter pilot hovered close to the mountain slope, a harness was lowered, and he was raised into the helicopter and flown directly to the hospital in the Rhône valley in fifteen minutes. Two weeks later, wiser, poorer, and acclimatized, he quickly climbed to the Matterhorn's 4,650-meter summit. Apart from these obvious acute anoxic symptoms, there are other, more insidious effects. During World War II the pilots flying from India to China "over the hump" of the Himalayan range frequently became disoriented by inoperative oxygen supply systems. Experienced pilots made bizarre decisions, sometimes resulting in narrowly averted disasters. And I've known brilliant academics, experienced mountaineers, who made ridiculous misjudgments during high-altitude climbs and paid for them with their lives.

The history of the ascent of Mount Everest is a story of misfortune as well as triumph. The conditions on Everest can become horrific. The disaster that occurred on May 10, 1996, in which eight climbers died when a blinding snowstorm suddenly enveloped the mountain, is only the most recent of a string of similar events. Sustained slopes of ice, avalanche-prone traverses, temperatures forty degrees below zero, and 100-mile-per-hour winds can create grave dangers. But climbers face another peril—cognitive deficits induced by hypoxia. In contrast to most ascents in the Alps of Europe, the 8,000-meter high peaks of the Himalaya cannot be climbed in one steady ascent. The "normal" route to the summit of Everest from the Nepal side of the mountain is a three-month-long endeavor.

In the Himalaya the mountain that one hopes to climb is usually several days to several weeks away from the nearest inhabited village. The mountain villages of Nepal, India, and Pakistan are furthermore not linked by roads to the cities in the plains below. In most regions of Nepal no wheeled vehicles, whatsoever, exist. Everything must be carried on the back of an animal or person. Indeed, in many areas the trails linking villages are too rough and steep for animals, and commerce depends on human porters who carry loads exceeding one hundred pounds. The climbing team must arrange for the transport of hundreds of pounds of food, kerosene or bottled gas to fuel stoves above the snow line, tents, clothing, and equipment. Everest Base Camp, the staging point for most expeditions climbing the normal route established by the Swiss and British expeditions of 1954 is higher than the summit of Mont Blanc, the highest mountain in western Europe. It takes about two weeks to acclimatize fully to the 5,300-meter altitude of Everest Base Camp, which is sited on the 300-meter-deep Khumbu Glacier and is shielded from the snow avalanches that thunder down at roughly three-hour intervals.

From Base Camp the climbers and Sherpa high-altitude porters first must bridge the crevasses of the icefall, the climb's first obstacle. The icefall is really the tongue of a glacier that flows down over a 300-meter-high cliff. The crevasses and "seracs," (small ice mounts) of the icefall continually shift, and a Sherpa team usually is assigned to keep the route open. The Sherpas are a

Tibetan people who migrated over the mountain border into Nepal about 300 years ago. The term *porter* doesn't convey what they do on a climb. They must climb the route using crampons (metal spikes attached to climbing boots), ice axes, and all the paraphernalia of extreme-altitude climbing, carrying fifty-pound loads. Members of the climbing team and the Sherpas generally first carry up drums of climbing rope and hundreds of "ice screws," which are used to set up "fixed ropes" along the route. The climbers can then hold on to the fixed ropes by means of clamping devices. Tents, food, fuel, radios, sleeping bags, and medical and oxygen supplies must all be carried up.

Eventually an "advanced base camp" (Camp Two) is erected on a relatively sheltered location at 6,300 meters. From there fixed ropes are set up and supplies are ferried to Camp Three at 7,150 meters, and to the usual, uppermost, 8,000-meter-high Camp Four on the South Col. Neither the expedition members nor the Sherpas generally use supplementary oxygen until they reach Camp Four, where it is sometimes necessary to use a slow flow rate in order to sleep restfully. The effects of altitude on physical activity are obvious and immediate. A normal climbing pace at 7,000 meters can mean taking one step upward and then pausing for ten seconds before taking another step. There are individual and group differences. The Sherpas who live year-round in villages like Pangboche, at 4,000 meters, generally are more fit than lowlanders. There is some evidence of a "sensitive period" for altitude acclimatization. Children of lowland parents who live at high altitudes during the first three years of life appear to be able to extract more oxygen from thin air than their lowland parents. They need to pass roughly half as much air through their lungs to work at the same level of effort.[14]

After everything is in place at Camp Four, the climbers who have best adapted to the altitude push ahead to the summit, climbing an additional 850 meters. Most climbers, team members and Sherpas alike, use supplementary oxygen for this final push. It generally takes fit climbers sixteen hours to reach the summit and return, exhausted, to Camp Four. For some appreciation of the more obvious effects of altitude, note that the "normal" 1,600-meter round-trip ascent and descent from the Swiss Alpine Club's Hörnli Hütte to the summit of the Matterhorn, which involves almost continuous rock climbing, takes eight or nine hours. An effect of the altitude that is not immediately apparent is the deterioration in cognition that has undoubtedly contributed to the fatalities on Everest and other 8,000-meter mountains. In the 1993 spring climbing season when we conducted our experiments on Everest, eight climbers died; sixty made it to the summit and back.

Strange lapses in thinking occur. On our expedition one of the members of the climbing team on his return from the summit came to the edge of a crevasse on the icefall that had been bridged by a ladder four weeks earlier. The ladder wasn't there, so he prepared to attempt to jump across. He had thrown his pack across the seven-foot-wide gap and was off to a running start in his heavy climbing boots and crampons when one of the Sherpas fortunately stopped him, shouting, "What you do!" The ladder had been moved about fifteen feet to the right by the icefall team. We were lucky; other expeditions have been wiped out on traverses on avalanche-prone slopes immediately after heavy snowfalls—conditions that are no-go for experienced mountaineers. On May 10, 1996, veteran mountaineers behaved bizarrely. Jon Krakauer describes an experienced professional mountain guide, "in the throes of his oxygen starved dementia," insisting that full oxygen bottles were empty. The guide later led a group of climbers past the safety of their tents, which were placed thirty yards away; two subsequently died. Indeed, the deaths of the first men to die on Everest, Leigh Mallory and Andrew Irvine, may have been caused by a failure of judgment. Though they were attempting to reach the summit and knew by then how long the final ascent would take, they left their flashlights behind in their final high camp.

The procedures that we used to assess the effects of hypoxia on Everest were similar to those that we had previously used to study Parkinson's disease.[15] Neurophysiological research had already established the fact that basal ganglia were among the brain structures most sensitive to oxygen deprivation. At Base

Camp we administered a battery of speech, syntax, and cognitive tests to five climbing members of the 1993 American Sagarmatha Expedition, after they had become fully acclimatized to the altitude. The tests were then run again as they first reached each progressively higher camp, and at their return to Base Camp after reaching Everest's summit. The experimenters stayed at Base Camp throughout the climb and used Motorola VHF radios to record speech samples and test results. Sony microsized digital tape recorders were used to ensure accurate measurements of time. Conventional analog tape recorders can slow down when their batteries become cold. Dr. Michael Sinclair performed the test routine on Everest at 7,150 meters above sea level—surely the highest location for any formal linguistic experiment. The test was photographed by Dr. Mark Rabold, who was securely anchored to the icy slope. Both Rabold and Sinclair reached the summit of Everest and safely returned.

We found that the timing of VOT became less controlled as the climbers ascended. The mean VOT interval that separated [b]s from [p]s, [d]s from [t]s, and [g]s from [k]s decreased from 26.0 to 6.4 ms between Base Camp and Camp Three; the VOT separation width "recovered" when the climbers returned to Base Camp after they had attained the summit. The climbers were arguably most exhausted at this point, ruling out fatigue as the major causal factor. The test of the comprehension of syntax that we used was originally designed to test hearing-impaired children at the Rhode Island School for the Deaf, one of the foremost institutions of its kind in the world. The test, devised by Betty and Trigg Engen, uses words that six-year-old English-speaking children understand. The types of sentences vary in syntactic complexity, but have the same number of words. The time that it took to understand simple sentences that six-year-old children comprehend increased 54 percent as the climbers ascended from Base Camp to Camp Three. Comprehension time also recovered at Base Camp immediately after the climb.

Figure 5-3 shows a typical sentence and the task; the subject had to say the number of the sketch that best matched the meaning of the sentence. The correlation coefficient between the

"The cat is sleeping on the bed."

"The boy is sick."

"The woman is giving tho nurse the baby."

5-3—Sentence Comprehension Task

This simple sentence/picture matching task became increasingly difficult for climbers as they reached progressively higher camps on Mount Everest. Response times increased 50 percent for these sentences, which six-year-old children readily comprehend. The test was originally devised by Trigg and Betty Engen for use with hearing-impaired children. It has since been used in many studies of aphasia and Parkinson's disease and for subjects with other neurological problems. (Courtesy of Trygg and Betty Engen)

decrease in VOT separation width and the increase in time that it took to comprehend simple sentences was -0.774, meaning that the increase in time required for cognition and the loss of speech motor control were highly related, which is what we would expect if the neural circuits regulating speech motor control and syntax shared the same neuroanatomical structures. Statistical tests showed that the possibility that this effect had occurred by chance was less than 1 in 10,000. The battery of cognitive tests that we administered showed no decrements, except for one climber who had a respiratory infection at Camp Three and had to descend. His VOTs overlapped and sentence comprehension time increased; we analyzed his results independently, but they conform to those of the other climbing members. None of the deficits were as severe as those in Parkinson's disease or aphasia, but it must be kept in mind that they occurred in individuals who cannot have been otherwise seriously impaired, since they were able to climb Mount Everest. The results, like the pattern of deficits associated with Parkinson's disease and Broca's aphasia, again suggest a linkage between the neural mechanisms implicated in speech motor control and syntax.

The technique that we used on Everest is being refined to see whether the cognitive performance of people engaged in critical tasks, such as pilots and air traffic controllers, can be monitored remotely by means of automatic computer-implemented speech analysis. It would be useful to be able to monitor people in situations where they may be exposed to carbon monoxide gas, which results in anoxia, fatigue, or other conditions that may impair or slow down their judgment. The techniques could also be useful in the diagnosis and treatment of Parkinson's disease.

Working Memory—
How Brain Mechanisms for
Speech Production
Facilitate Comprehension

Alan Baddeley, a young psychologist then working at Yale University, in the 1970s provided one of the clues for the link between speech production and the comprehension of syntax that is apparent in Broca's aphasia, Parkinson's disease, and high-altitude anoxia. In his influential 1986 book, *Working Memory,* Baddeley presented the results of a series of experiments that indicated that as we attempt to comprehend the meaning of a sentence we temporarily hold the stream of incoming words in a verbal memory store in our brain. It is clear that any final decision on the meaning of a sentence must be deferred until we hear or read the entire sentence. Although we can immediately begin to put the meaning of a sentence together as we hear the first few words, in many cases the syntactic structure of a sentence and the particular meaning of each word are not evident until the end of the sentence. For example, the first three words of the sentence "The witness examined by the lawyer shocked the jury" could have been the start of the sentence "The witness examined the evidence". The word *witness,* in that case, would be the actor, the subject of the sentence who did the examining rather than the person who was examined.

Words also generally have different meanings that often can be inferred only when we know the context in which they occur. A reader might be certain that the sentence "Albert slammed the dogs home to seal the ship's watertight bulkheads" described an instance of animal abuse if his comprehension of the sentence's meaning was not deferred until its end.[16] Baddeley proposed that the mechanism by which we keep words active in working memory was "articulatory rehearsal," a sort of "silent speech" in which the motor gestures that would have produced the words were modeled by means of the neural structures that regulate these gestures when we talk. The experimental data on which Baddeley based this theory showed that subjects had more difficulty recalling lists of longer words than lists of shorter words, which is what would be expected if the articulatory rehearsal mechanism had a finite capacity. When articulatory rehearsal was impeded by having a subject say unrelated words aloud, both the comprehension of syntax and the number of words that he or she could recall decreased. Many independent experiments have since replicated and confirmed Baddeley's theory. People comprehend the meaning of a sentence in verbal working memory, where they consider the syntactic properties and semantic associations of each word, as well as the context in which they hear or read a sentence.[17] One of the key elements of the process is the articulatory rehearsal mechanism, which maintains words in verbal working memory.

PET Studies of Verbal Working Memory

Neurophysiological studies of human subjects confirm the link between articulatory rehearsal using brain mechanisms involved in speech motor control and the comprehension of syntax. By means of positron emission tomography (PET), Karin Stromswold of Rutgers University and her colleagues studied neurologically intact subjects whose task was to state whether sentences that differed with respect to their syntactic complexity and/or the presence of non-words were "acceptable." The study found greater metabolic activity in Broca's area when subjects read sentences containing a center-embedded relative clause than when they read sentences containing a right-branching clause. Relative values of metabolic activity were obtained by subtracting PET data for center-embedded sentences such as "The juice that the child spilled stained the rug" from similar right-branching sentences such as "The child spilled the juice that stained the rug." As Stromswold et al. (1996) and many previous studies note, center-embedded sentences appear to be more difficult to comprehend because they place a greater load on working-memory, since resolution of the initial noun is delayed until the intervening clause is processed.

However, it is impossible syntactically to process a sentence without identifying its words and their syntactic constraints, for example, whether a particular verb can take a direct object or not. William Croft's 1991 book, *Syntactic Categories and Grammatical Relations,* makes this clear. This information cannot be recovered from the neural lexicon unless the words of a sentence are maintained in working memory. In this light, the data of an independent

1996 PET study by Edward Awh and his colleagues at the University of Michigan definitively demonstrate that neurologically intact subjects use neural structures implicated in speech production subvocally to "rehearse" letters of the alphabet, maintaining them in working memory. Subtractions of PET activity showed increased metabolic activity in the parts of the brain that are active when we talk when PET data from a task involving verbal working memory were compared with a task that had a substantially lower working-memory load. Increased activity was found in neuroanatomical structures known to be implicated in regulating speech production: Broca's area, premotor cortex, supplementary motor area, cerebellum, and anterior cingulate gyrus. Since all of these cortical areas form parts of circuits involving subcortical basal ganglia, we can see why speech production and sentence comprehension deficits co-occur in aphasia, Parkinson's disease, and anoxia, in which the brain mechanisms regulating speech production are impaired—these phenomena all suggest that the brain mechanisms that regulate speech production are involved in the rehearsal mechanism that maintains words in verbal working memory.

Putting the data of these neurophysiological, aphasia, hypoxia, and Parkinson's disease studies together, we obtain a clearer picture. The neural bases of human speech motor control and syntax appear to be linked together in a functional language system that produces and comprehends spoken language.[18] At least some of the neuroanatomical structures that support the language system are also implicated in other aspects of cognition. Destruction or impaired activity in these parts of the brain can therefore result in marked deficits in motor control, comprehension, and cognition.

Nature and Nurture

Virtually all linguists note that a "critical" or "sensitive" period exists in which children effortlessly acquire the ability both to perform the motor acts necessary to speak a dialect with a "native" accent and to master the "rules" of syntax and morphology. This is one of the phenomena that led Noam Chomsky and other linguists to propose that human beings have a detailed genetic "blueprint" for the possible rules of grammar of all languages. According to Chomsky, the human brain's "language organ" has a genetically transmitted blueprint, a hypothetical "universal grammar," that specifies the grammatical rules that can occur in any language. Children supposedly do not really have to learn the rules of grammar that govern what is acceptable in a particular language or dialect. Their internal blueprint is instead "triggered" by what they hear during the critical period.

Gilbert Gottlieb, a psychologist at the University of North Carolina, has shown that this theory holds for ducks. Ducks most likely have a genetically programmed "duck call" organ that is triggered during a critical period. Gottlieb played tape recordings of duck calls to duck eggs that were about to hatch. Several months later the ducklings, which were raised without hearing or seeing other ducks, began to make appropriate duck calls. In contrast, eggs raised to maturity that were not exposed to duck calls resulted in ducklings that produced aberrant quacks. The Chomskian theory of universal grammar, in essence, claims a similar neural basis for the grammars of human languages. However, there is abundant evidence that the neural circuits that regulate most aspects of human behavior are learned, often within a "sensitive" or "critical" period.

Again, most of the present "hard" evidence consists of electrophysiological data on motor control and the perception of vision and sound in monkeys and other animals. In brief, these studies show that the general neural substrate that allows an animal to acquire particular behavioral traits is genetically transmitted. Extremely fast reaction times enable cats to coordinate vision and paw movements to seize prey. People have a neural system that permits them to speak and comprehend language. However, these neural systems offer the *potential* for behavior. The neural circuits that regulate complex aspects of behavior are shaped by exposure to an individual's environment within a sensitive period. Neuroanatomical experiments on cats, for example, show that inputs to visual cortex develop in early life in accordance with visual input.

Different visual inputs yield different input connections. For example, neurons in the visual cortical areas of young cats that have been deprived of vision from birth instead respond to auditory and tactile stimuli.[19] Behavioral data indicate that similar processes account for the formation of such basic aspects of vision as depth perception in human children. Cross-eyed children do not develop normal depth perception, because their eyes do not present their developing visual cortex with properly aligned images. The neural bases of depth perception depend on a complex reorganization of the brain in response to the images that a young child or kitten sees. If young brains are not exposed to vision within a certain critical period, these neural processes never occur. This process, in which the neural circuits that structure, say, a child's or a kitten's visual perception are formed as inactive neurons die, has been termed "neural Darwinism" by Gerald Edelman (1987). Edelman's comprehensive review of the data of hundreds of studies points out a metaphorical "struggle for existence" in which neuronal pathways that are not used deteriorate.

Direct evidence for the human brain's representation of skilled motor-cognitive tasks is beginning to become available. Functional magnetic resonance imaging (FMRI) allows neuroscientists to view the brain activity associated with particular activities in different parts of the body. Playing a stringed instrument such as a violin or a viola requires that the digits of the fingers of the left hand continually execute precise controlled maneuvers. The second to fifth digits ply the strings pressing lightly or hard, while the thumb grasps the neck of the instrument and changes its position and the pressure that it exerts. Proficient musicians generally are persons who started to play stringed instruments when they were young. In a clever FMRI study involving scientists and musicians in Germany and the United States, the digits of nine adult musicians and six nonmusicians were stimulated while brain activity was mapped.[20] The areas of the cerebral cortex that responded to digit stimulation were greater in the musicians and occupied a somewhat different location. No differences were observed in the representation of the right digits of the musicians and nonmusicians. Furthermore, there was a clear relation between the size of the area of cortical representation of the musicians' left digits and the age at which they had started to learn to play their instruments. The cortical areas corresponding to left-digit sensory information were about 70 percent greater in the musicians who had started to play before the age of twelve years. That is about the age at which children begin to approach adult levels of competence in both their ability to produce the complex articulatory maneuvers necessary to produce human speech and their ability to comprehend sentences that have complex syntax.[21]

Wild Children

Human parents usually do not deliberately isolate children from contact with language, so it is difficult to assess the effects of the environment on the brain bases of linguistic ability. The case of Genie is an exception, although the almost complete isolation of this unfortunate girl from virtually all of the sensory and emotional events of childhood confounds the issue. When Genie was twenty months old, she was shut in a dingy room, strapped to a potty chair during the day, placed in a straitjacket at night, and never talked to. The windows were blacked out, so she could at most see a portion of the sky and a nearby house. Her psychotic father and his intimidated son "communicated" with her in doglike barks and growls. At the age of thirteen and a half Genie was liberated. Her father shot himself, and she was delivered into the hands of a group of psychologists and linguists who attempted to rehabilitate her. Susan Curtiss's 1977 account of Genie's subsequent progress is arguably the best-documented account of how almost total social, linguistic, and environmental deprivation affects the development of human linguistic and cognitive ability.

Despite three years of intensive language exercise, Genie rarely spoke; instruction in sign language, therefore, was attempted. When she did speak, it was in a labored, inarticulate manner. Unfortunately no objective acoustic analyses of Genie's speech were made, so we do not know the precise nature of her speech production deficits. There is no evidence that she comprehended English syntax; she was unable to grasp the meaning of a sentence without extralinguistic contextual cues and gestures. She did acquire a reasonably extensive vocabulary, which she combined in two- and three-word utterances that sometimes conformed to the syntactic rules of English, sometimes not. Genie had clearly passed the critical period for the acquisition of normal linguistic ability. One of the major issues concerning Genie's inability to acquire normal competence was whether she was also mentally retarded. The implicit assumption was Chomsky's claim that the neural bases of language and cognition are independent. However, it is inherently impossible to differentiate the effects of extreme deprivation on language and thought, since many of the neuroanatomical structures that regulate language are also implicated in other aspects of cognition. Genie's language deficits appear to be quite similar to those noted more than 150 years earlier for Victor the "wild child of Aveyron," who was found wandering in the woods, possibly raised with animals. The description of Victor's language by his tutor Professor Itard is strikingly similar to that of Genie.

Toy Linguistics

Paradoxically, the primary evidence that Chomskian linguists cite to support their claim that an inborn universal grammar exists is the failure of the algorithmic approach similar to digital computer programs. As Ray Jackendoff notes in his book *Patterns in the Mind: Language and Human Nature,* which presents the Chomskian position, "Thousands of linguists throughout the world have been trying for decades to figure out the principles behind the grammatical patterns of various languages. . . . But any linguist will tell you that we are nowhere near a complete account of the mental grammar for any language" (Jackendoff 1994, 26). Over the past forty years it has become apparent that linguists following Chomsky's principles have produced a sort of toy linguistics. Despite decades of intensive effort only a small subset of the sentences of any language can be described by means of syntactic rules. These sentences typically are the examples presented to demonstrate the power of this algorithmic method in introductory courses and expository texts such as Jackendoff's book and Steven Pinker's 1994 book, *The Language Instinct.* As the linguistic corpus expands, the number of putative rules begins to approach the number of sentences. The rules of grammar become torturously complex and ultimately fail. Charles Gross in 1979 showed that the algorithmic approach failed for a fragment of the grammar of Parisian French; subsequent failures have been unreported.[22] The limits of algorithmic descriptions of behavior have been noted in other domains of science, for instance, by neurophysiologists studying motor control. However, no one would claim that the instruction set for bolting a bumper in place on a Toyota is innate because thousands of experts have been unable to make industrial robots as adaptable as human beings. Yet that is precisely the linguistic argument. It first notes that generative linguists have failed to adequately describe any language. It then notes that children acquire language and concludes that the principles underlying language must therefore be innate.

The Chomskian position also holds that all aspects of the innate neural language module exist only in human beings. While it is apparent that some aspects of human linguistic ability are not present in any other living species, that position is too extreme. Some proponents of Chomsky's theories tilt the playing field toward human uniqueness. Steven Pinker, for example, in his recent book (p. 262) correctly cites experimental data that show that human infants categorically perceive the VOT differences that distinguish the voiced consonants [b], [d], and [g] from their unvoiced counterparts [p], [t], and [k]. What Pinker fails to note is Patricia Kuhl's experiments at the University of Washington that demonstrated that chinchillas and monkeys also perceive these sound contrasts as well as other linguistic distinctions in like manner. Kuhl's work is well known to cognitive scientists and psychologists who study human language. The innate mechanisms present in humans, monkeys, and rodents appear to be a property of the mammalian auditory system and the associative properties of the brain. Even small mammalian brains are capable of drawing inferences from repeated presentations of auditory signals that are meaningful. Kuhl's chinchillas quickly learned that they received tasty food rewards when they pushed a bar on hearing a [b] or a [d].

In fact, Brad Seebach and his colleagues at Brown University have shown that a computer simulation of an "associative neural network"[23] (one of the current models of the brain's computational structure) could also "learn" to identify the sounds [b], [d], [g], [p], [t], and [k]. Seebach "trained" his model by exposing it to syllables having the form [ba], [da], [ga] and enunciated by one male speaker. Seebach took care to use speech samples that differed from each other; no person produces the exact same speech signal every time she or he says the "same" word. The simple computer network, really a toy model of the brain of even a chinchilla, given the number of neurons in a rodent's brain, quickly learned to categorize these sounds. It in essence extracted the "prototypes" of the sounds, automatically factoring out the variations between each speech sample. The computer network, without further training, then was exposed to the [ba], [da], [ga], [p], and so forth of a second male and a female speaker. It was also able to identify their sounds correctly.

Paul Churchland, a philosopher of science, in his 1995 book, *The Engine of Reason, the Seat of the Soul: A Philosophical Journey into the Brain*, argues that grammar is acquired by associative neural networks. Churchland is a member of the faculty of the University of California at San Diego, a center for the study of associative neural networks. Stevan Harnad, the editor in chief of a leading scientific journal in this field, *Behavioral and Brain Sciences,* correctly points out that present computer simulations of the associative neural networks that may exist in biological brains are indeed toy models. They have only a minuscule fraction of the associative properties of a real brain. The point that Harnad completely misses is that despite the limited computational powers of present computer models compared with human brains, these toy models are nonetheless capable of acquiring the limited demonstrations of grammar that Chomskian linguists cite.

In his review of Churchland's recent book, Harnad notes that "Churchland misconstrues [a] particular toy model of a tiny fragment of grammar, taking it to be a refutation of Chomsky's evidence and arguments for an unlearnable, hence inborn, universal grammar." Harnad's characterization of computer-simulated neural nets as "tiny toy demonstrations" applies with equal force to the linguistic researches that he refers to, which never exceed "a tiny fragment of grammar."

The evidence cited by Chomsky and many other linguists first of all consists of a few rules in one language and a few in another. No grammar has ever been presented that even approaches the full range of phenomena found in *any* single language. Although Chomsky continually claims that he has isolated "linguistic universals" that apply to all languages, no such entities have been demonstrated. On closer inspection, one learns that they apply to an ill-defined "core grammar." The part of language that Chomskian methods cannot account for is labeled the "peripheral grammar."[24] This distinction, in itself, makes it impossible to test the theory. However, the inherent methodological deficiency of the Chomskian enterprise is the claim that syntax is a set of rules built into the human brain that are independent of meaning. In fact, many linguists have gone beyond this formal paradigm. William Croft in his groundbreaking 1991 book, *Syntactic Categories and Grammatical Relations*, for example, shows that the basic, well-attested, universal categories of human language, such as nouns and verbs, cannot be defined by means of the formal algorithmic apparatus of Chomskian linguistic theory. Nouns and verbs ultimately refer to the real world, things and actions.

The claim that children must have inborn knowledge of syntax to acquire language also rests on the assumption that a child is a little Chomsky, proposing and solving algorithms. The power of cognitive processes like associative learning and imitation is routinely ignored in many theoretical discussions of language acquisition. Steven Pinker's discussion of a deaf child acquiring American Sign Language (ASL) from parents who are imperfect models is a good example of a Chomskian treatment of language acquisition.

Linguists continually stress the fact that the children learn the correct rules of grammar, though they often hear imperfect, incomplete speech. Anyone who has ever attempted to transcribe the tape-recorded proceedings of a conference knows that virtually no one speaks in grammatical sentences. But most people somehow know what constitutes a grammatical sentence. How, then, do children ever acquire the grammar of their language or dialect? In most cases we simply don't have a complete record of the speech that a child hears, so it is difficult to test this part of Chomskian theory. However, one recent study that Jenny Singleton and Elissa Newport completed at the University of Illinois has allowed us to test this proposition. In contrast to most developmental studies of language acquisition, theirs knew the language input to the deaf child they studied, for it was limited to the ASL produced by his deaf parents, who were imperfect signers. If Chomsky is correct, then the child should have "extracted" the correct rules of ASL grammar even though his parents made systematic errors. Whereas the child's parents, who were the models for the child, made errors 40 percent of the time for certain ASL signs, the child had a 20 percent error rate. These data have been interpreted as evidence for universal grammar. Pinker (1994, 38–39) claims that this demonstrates that the child had innate knowledge of the underlying principles, because otherwise he could not have performed better than his parents. However, Pinker relates only part of the data. He fails to note that the child had a higher error rate than his parents when they incorrectly modeled other ASL signs more than 50 percent of the time. Therefore, the child does *not* acquire the "correct" rules supposedly coded in a hypothetical innate syntax organ. The complete data refute the Chomskian model; the deaf child appears to be making use of the associative cognitive processes that allow pigeons, dogs, and humans to abstract general principles from specific occurrences. He picks the form that is used most often, whether it is "grammatical" or not. Therefore, the deaf boy's ASL signs are consistent with his learning syntax by means of the process of associative learning (imperfectly modeled in simulated distributed neural nets).

A 1996 study of normal hearing infants in which Elissa Newport participated demonstrates even more forcefully that children rapidly learn the principles of human language by means of associative processes. Jenny Saffran, Richard Aslin, and Newport showed that eight-month-old infants can learn to segment the acoustic signals that specify the words of an artificial spoken language after two minutes. The words of any human language are ⌐ made up of syllables. Since normal speech is composed of a sequence of words, sequences of syllables that constitute words will occur more often than sequences that do not constitute real words. Therefore, a neural network that makes use of associative learning can determine the sound patterns that constitute the words of a language from the statistical pattern without reference to meaning—the syllable sequences that constitute words will occur more often. Saffran and her colleagues at the University of Rochester showed that the infants who listened to sound sequences in which certain syllables were regularly joined together to form pseudo-words responded differentially to the pseudo-words compared to syllable sequences that did not constitute pseudo-words. The test procedure monitored the time that infants spent listening to sound patterns after their two-minute learning experience. The infants spent more time listening to non-words than to the pseudo-words of the artificial language. No innate knowledge of possible word structure was necessary; general associative learning sufficed.[25]

The Language Gene

If you have been following the current debate on the brain bases of language, you may have read that evidence for a "language gene" has been found that "proves" Chomsky's theory. The studies of Myrna Gopnik and her colleagues at McGill University, which have been cited by Chomsky and his advocates, claim that a genetically transmitted, grammar-specific deficit exists in about half of the male and female members of a large family (KE) of four generations. The afflicted members of this family supposedly had high error rates in comprehending regular English constructions, such as the regular past tense of verbs (*walked* versus *walk*), but were uncompromised on irregular verbs (*run* versus *ran*). The cognitive and speech production abilities of afflicted members of this family were claimed to be similar to those of unafflicted siblings. The history surrounding this research is interesting. Gopnik on a visit to London viewed a short BBC Television film documenting an ongoing study by a British research group directed by Faraneh Vargha-Khadem of the Institute of Child Health in London and Richard Passingham at the University of Oxford. The television segment showed children whose speech was so distorted and incomprehensible that English subtitles were used. Gopnik contacted the family and administered a short set of tests that appeared to show these specific linguistic deficits.

However, though a genetically transmitted disorder (probably involving a non-sex-linked autosomal dominant gene) affects half of the members of family KE, their speech, language, and cognitive deficits transcend the generation of specific rules of grammar. The comprehensive 1995 study by Vargha-Khadem and her colleagues shows that the afflicted family members have

> impaired processing and expression of other aspects of grammar, grossly defective articulation of speech sounds, and . . . in addition the affected family members have both Verbal and Performance IQ scores that are on average 18–19 points below those of the unaffected members. This psychological profile indicates that the inherited disorder does not affect morphosyntax [past tense and plural words] exclusively, or even primarily; rather it affects intellectual, linguistic, and orofacial praxic functions generally. The evidence from the KE family thus provides no support for the proposed existence of grammar-specific genes. (Vargha-Khadem et al. 1995, 930)

To conclude, like the brains of other animals, the human brain appears to have a unique system that is adapted to regulate a particular behavior, spoken language, that greatly contributes to our

biological fitness. However, the neural structure and general architecture of this unique human functional language system conforms
to the physiological principles that shape unique functional systems adapted to other behaviors that exist in other species. It is not
fully specified by a genetic "blueprint." Its structure is not logical
or economical, and its neuroanatomical components are involved
in the regulation of other aspects of behavior.

The data currently available point to a human functional language system in which the neural mechanisms that regulate speech
production play a central role. We appear to pull words out of the
brain's dictionary by means of the sound pattern that is the "name"
of the word. We maintain words in verbal working memory by
means of subvocal speech in which at least some of the neural
mechanisms that regulate speech production play an active part. We
comprehend the meaning of a sentence by considering the meaning of its words, the syntax of the sentence, and any other information we can bring to bear on the problem. All this takes place in a
neural system that consists of circuits that link neurons in different
neuroanatomical entities. These include the traditional sites of language, Broca's and Wernicke's areas, but many other parts of the
brain are active when we talk or comprehend the meaning of an
utterance or written text. And though the basic architecture of this
functional language system clearly is part of our human genetic
endowment, the details of syntax, speech, and the words of the languages that a person knows appear to be learned by means of the
associative processes that enable us to learn other complex aspects
of behavior. However, we must remember that we stand on the
threshold of an understanding of how brains really work. The great-
est danger perhaps rests in making claims that are not supported by
data or that inherently cannot be subjected to rigorous tests.

CHAPTER 6

What, When, and Where Did Eve Speak to Adam, and He to Her?

HE ANSWERS TO THE QUESTIONS in the chapter title all hinge on *which* Adam and Eve you're thinking of. In the five-million-year-long lineage that connects us to the common ancestors of apes and human beings, there have been many Adams and many Eves.

In the beginning there was the word, but the vocal communications of our most distant hominid ancestors five million years or so ago probably didn't really differ from those of the ape-hominid ancestor. Most of their cries would have been linked to emotion and instinct. And as Chapter 2 noted, the ability to produce vocalizations that are *not* linked to emotion and instinct seems to create the gulf between human language and the vocal communications of apes. Whereas we can produce a chorus of changing formant frequency patterns that signal concepts abstract and concrete, apes are bound to simple melodies tied to mood. Nonetheless, there are some common elements in human and ape vocal communication that may have been the jumping-off point for human speech. Formant frequency patterns, which are the key to human speech, also play a part in primate vocal communication. Indeed, these patterns probably play a part in *all* mammal vocal communication.

Until recently, animal vocal communication was thought to depend exclusively on modulations of the voice's pitch. The pitch of your voice depends on the rate at which the vocal cords of your larynx open and close. And since the larynx is not very different in a monkey, a chimpanzee, or a human, pitch variations convey emotion in primates. Charles Darwin's 1872 book, *The Expression of the Emotions in Man and Animals,* is the theoretical framework for many current studies of animal communication. Darwin correctly noted that the human voice conveys our emotions, independent of language, independent of will. When my cousin telephoned me some months ago, I instantly knew that something terrible had happened, before he told me that his wife's sister had been killed when their car spun out of control on their return from a wedding. The "tone"—the pitch, laryngeal quality, and inflection—of his voice conveyed tragedy. Pitch does convey emotion. Thanassi Protopappas, a cognitive scientist at Brown University, and I found that a high fundamental frequency of phonation (the acoustic "correlate" of pitch) signaled the terror expressed in the voice of a helicopter pilot as he signaled desperately for emergency-landing clearance as the helicopter rotor was disintegrating.[1]

But it has become evident that other aspects of speech, including the formant frequency patterns that convey the sounds of language, are implicated in human and animal "non-linguistic" communication. One process absolutely necessary in the perception of human speech is the neural calculation that allows us to determine the length of the supralaryngeal vocal tract (SVT) that is producing the speech signal we are listening to. As was noted earlier, the vowel [i] (the vowel of *see*) is optimal for this purpose, but other sounds will work, albeit with more potential for confusion. For many years I thought the capacity for this process of "vocal tract normalization" was innate and specifically human. The first premise appears to be correct, since some three-month-old children, when they imitate the sounds of their parents, produce sounds that are not direct imitations of their parents' formant frequencies (that would be impossible, since their parents' SVTs are more than twice as long), but frequency-scaled formant frequencies. So an infant's imitation of his mother's vowels will have formant frequencies that are twice as high, *because* they must "sound" the same to the infant.[2]

However, the second premise is incorrect; it is not only humans who can estimate the length of a vocal tract from the formant frequencies of a vocalization. W. Tecumseh Fitch's brilliant Brown University Ph.D. thesis shows that chimpanzees and various species of monkeys can do this. Dogs and other mammals also probably can derive vocal tract size from formant frequencies. Fitch demonstrated that many animals signal how big they are (or deceptively signal how big they would like to appear) by means of formant frequency patterns. A longer supralaryngeal airway will produce lower formant frequencies (just as a longer organ pipe has a lower "tone"); larger animals generally have longer supralaryngeal airways, and formant frequencies become an important auditory cue for the size of the animal or person vocalizing. In situations involving potential conflict, animals make themselves appear bigger—dogs and monkeys, for example, increase their visual size by raising their fur or hair. Dogs also make themselves "sound" bigger by keeping their muzzles closed, even when they bare their teeth to snarl. The almost closed mouth produces lower formant frequencies than an open mouth. Apes and monkeys likewise generate aggressive sounds with their lips protruding and partly closed. The open-mouthed "fear grins" of apes, in contrast, result in higher formant frequencies.

We humans continue to use formant frequency patterns to signal size differences unrelated to the "linguistic" content of a message. In human society male speech is differentiated from female speech by lower formant frequencies, which come from longer male supralaryngeal airways, as well as lower pitch, due to the larger adult male larynx. But humans improve on nature in signaling gender vocally. Most little boys unconsciously learn to talk with their lips somewhat pursed, which gives them lower formant frequencies, even though their airways are not longer than those of little girls. I became aware of this effect many years ago when I thought that our six-year-old son precociously had a girlfriend. It turned out that one of his playmates was a little boy who had four older sisters—the six-year-old boy had imitated the speech patterns of his sisters producing "girl talk." The acoustic "cue" that marked his speech as little "girl talk" was the formant frequencies of his vowels. Jacqueline Sachs, Donna Erikson, and I recorded five-year-old boys and girls.[3] We found that the pitch of their voices was about the same, which should not be surprising if one remembers that boys' voices change at puberty, when the larynx usually becomes disproportionately larger in males. The vocal tracts of adult males, too, are longer than those of adult females. However, it is also apparent that the actual lengths of the supralaryngeal vocal tracts of five-year-old boys are not generally longer than those of five-year-old girls. We found that the children were modeling their speech on adult prototypes. The little boys were talking with their lips pursed to a greater extent than the girls. Lip "rounding," which involves pushing your lips forward and closer together, produces lower format frequencies. The girls generally talked with a smile, their lips being retracted. They were "learning" the subtle female dialect of American English. Our 1972 paper also showed that the tomboys in our five-year-old subjects were identified as boys. Children obviously pick up these subtle behavioral distinctions of gender. Videotapes of five-year-olds conversing with "male doctor" and "female nurse" hand puppets showed lip shapes changing as they spoke for the male or female puppets.

It is likely that formant frequency patterns conveyed similar information in our earliest hominid ancestors. Lower formant frequencies could either intimidate adversaries or attract mates. The functions of formant frequency related to sexuality and power yielded auditory mechanisms sensitive to formant frequency patterns—the jumping-off point for the elaboration of formant frequency patterns for rapid human speech communication. Modifications of food call, which can be seen in a limited degree in present-day monkeys, also may have provided the behavioral context for increased biological fitness (more surviving children) for variations that yielded the possibility of conveying more information vocally.[4] *When* this happened is unclear. Given the linkage between the neural bases for precise manual motor control and voluntary speech that is apparent when the brains of modern human beings are damaged, and given the toolmaking abilities of *Homo erectus,* it is almost certain that some sort of voluntary speech that made use of controlled formant frequency patterns was in place by that epoch of hominid evolution, the penultimate stage of human evolution. Our cousins the Neanderthals surely possessed speech, though more susceptible to misinterpretation because of its acoustic properties, and language.

Anatomically Modern *Homo sapiens*

We can be virtually certain that efficient speech communication equivalent to our own was established in the earliest anatomically modern human beings. The skull of the modern Skhul V fossil who lived about 100,000 years ago *must* have supported a modern SVT, with a low larynx. As is the case for the skulls of normal living adult human beings, there simply is not enough room for a larynx positioned close to the nose, with a pharynx behind it (the monkey-chimpanzee-australopithecine configuration). The photographs in Figure 6-1 of the Skhul V fossil and the casts of its SVT and a modern human adult vocal tract show that this is so. William Howells's studies comparing the fossil skull with those of modern adults show that it falls within the modern human range of variation. His studies also indicate that classic Neanderthal skulls do not fall into the range of variation of modern human beings—one of his papers aptly used the term *monster* to describe the sort of creature that could have both Neanderthal and human features.

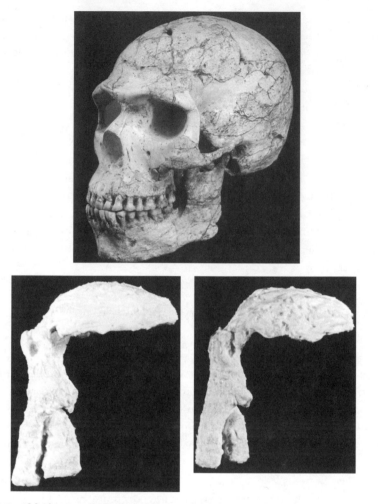

6-1—Skhul V Fossil Skull and SVT and Adult Human SVT

This anatomically modern human hominid, who lived about 100,000 years ago, had a modern human supralaryngeal vocal tract (SVT). A casting of the fossil SVT is pictured on the left; a modern human adult SVT, on the right. Both SVTs show the supralaryngeal airway in the position that would produce the vowel of the word *but*. (Adapted from Lieberman 1975; courtesy of Peabody Museum, Harvard University)

The earliest complete skulls of anatomically modern *Homo sapiens* date back to about 100,000 years ago. Skhul V and Jebel Qafzeh, whose remains were unearthed in Israel, were buried with ritual grave goods. This in itself points to cognitive and linguistic capabilities that could conceive of and communicate concepts such as death and perhaps life after death. This level of conceptual structure could have been communicated without talking by means of manual sign language.[5] That, of course, is how many contemporary deaf people communicate and presumably think of these and equally abstract concepts. However, the fact that Skhul V and Jebel Qafzeh had modern human vocal tracts shows that they talked.

The reason for this is perfectly obvious if you consider the *disadvantages* of having a modern vocal tract. The low position of our larynx makes it more likely for us to choke to death on food or liquids that obstruct the larynx or pass through the larynx into our lungs. As long ago as 1859 Darwin noted "the strange fact that every particle of food and drink we swallow has to pass over the orifice of the trachea, with some risk of falling into the lungs" (Darwin 1859, 191). When we swallow liquids or food, our tongue first vigorously propels them toward the back of our mouth. There the powerful pharyngeal constrictor muscles propel the mass of food or liquid downward, but it must enter the esophagus, not the larynx. People usually tuck their larynx forward as they swallow. The maneuver is only one of the complex gymnastic feats that we "unconsciously" execute when we eat and talk. But if your timing becomes uncoordinated, as it may after a few drinks, food or a combined liquid-food mass may end up in your larynx. The instructions discreetly placed in all restaurants for the Heimlich maneuver save the lives of an estimated ten thousand people a year in the United States alone. This maneuver pops open the stuffed larynx with the air blast that occurs when you squeeze below the victim's chest. In contrast, the nonhuman "standard plan" vocal tract described by the British anatomist Victor Negus maintains separate swallowing and air pathways for liquids and smaller pieces of solid food *before* food starts being propelled by the pharyngeal constrictor muscles. The nonhuman larynx is positioned before the pharyngeal constrictors. Most animals that swallow large pieces of food have to momentarily lower their larynx as the food makes its way into the pharynx. However, as Negus noted, the nonhuman larynx position is clearly better adapted for eating and drinking. The human SVT is *less* well adapted for ingesting liquids and soft food.

The human vocal tract has other liabilities. Our mouths and jaws are shorter than those of nonhuman primates.[6] If you compare a human jawbone and upper jaw with a Neanderthal's, it becomes obvious that there is lots of space for Neanderthal teeth. Neanderthals never had impacted wisdom teeth. Though our teeth are smaller than those of *Homo erectus* or Neanderthals, there is less room for them. Usually about 20 percent of the students in any of my classes have had their wisdom teeth removed. Before the invention of anesthesia, which was first used for dentistry in the mid-nineteenth century, extracting an impacted wisdom tooth (the third molar) was a formidable undertaking. Impacted teeth, a secondary consequence of our vocal tract, led to infections and death.

Since our upper and lower jaws are smaller than they would be if we really were Neanderthal-like creatures, there is another deficiency related to toothiness. We cannot chew food as efficiently as we could if we had greater tooth areas in contact when we chewed. Dentists concerned with the efficiency of false teeth have found that the most important factor is the "swept surface area" (the amount of grinding surface that comes into contact as we chew).[7] Sharp serrated teeth that the villains in James Bond films would have been proud to sport were tested on "chewing machines" that replicated the motions of deficient, normal, and somewhat supernormal human chewing patterns. Beyond a certain point the pressure exerted on the teeth did not really change chewing efficiency. So you don't need to grind your teeth while chewing. Nor did the sharpness of the false teeth have much effect, so razor-sharp false teeth will never come into fashion.

The net effect of chewing food thoroughly is a 5 to 10 percent increase in the absorption of nutrients from the average human diet. This does not seem like a great difference, but it provides an enormous "selective advantage" in evolutionary terms. Overweight populations in some countries are a recent phenomenon. In most parts of the world today, food shortages are still commonplace, and that was the case almost everywhere two hundred years ago. Under the conditions that prevailed until the start of the industrial revolution in Europe, almost everyone lived on the edge. A 5 percent advantage in sustaining life in the near-famine conditions of daily life would have been meaningful in the Darwinian struggle for existence. Indeed, as Darwin noted, the concept of the natural selection and the struggle for existence owes its existence to Thomas Malthus, whose *Essay on the Principle of Population* warned Europeans of impending doom as the result of a population explosion at the end of the eighteenth century. What Malthus did not envision was the enormous increase in agricultural productivity that occurred in the nineteenth century in the industrialized "first world."

Finally, as Victor Negus pointed out, the right-angle bend in the human vocal tract also reduces the respiratory efficiency of our upper airways. So we can conclude that having a human vocal tract with a low larynx increases our chances for immediate death by asphyxiation, increases the chances for a slower death by infection from impacted wisdom teeth, reduces the chances of survival when food supplies are limited (the "normal" condition for most people past and present), and restricts breathing to a degree. In fact, the *only* function that is better served is speech production. Specifically, the ability to produce sounds that enhance the process of formant frequency "decoding." But it should be abundantly clear by now that speech production entails having a brain that is capable of learning and regulating the voluntary motor commands that underlie speech. *There would have been no increase in biological fitness for the human vocal tract unless a human brain adapted for speech had existed in our immediate African ancestors!*

The Neanderthals, who had vocal tracts that were intermediate between ours and the ape-australopithecine model, are extinct. They illustrate both the continuity of evolution and the adaptive value of speech. Their speech was less efficient and "clear" than ours; they represent an intermediate stage in the evolution of human speech. Neanderthals must also have possessed the neural circuits and neuroanatomical structures that regulate speech production and that are implicated in human language and cognition. The genetic isolating effects of speech and the lesser communicative efficiency of the speech of Neanderthals may in itself account for their gradual extinction over the course of many generations. It is possible that although their brain was as large as our own, their neural substrate regulating speech, language, and cognition may have been less developed than our own. However, it is impossible to know whether linguistic and cognitive ability actually was less developed in Neanderthals than in our immediate ancestors. Archaeological studies that shed more light on the behavior of early humans and Neanderthals may resolve this question.

However, the presence of a human vocal tract in fossils such as SkhulV, Jebel Qafzeh, and other early humans who lived on the rim of the Mediterranean Sea 100,000 years ago is an *index*, a mark that they definitely had brains capable of regulating their vocal tracts. Given the non-speech liabilities of the human vocal tract, it is certain that our immediate ancestors had brains that, like ours, would have enabled them to regulate the complex articulatory maneuvers that underlie speech. And we have seen that the brain mechanisms that are implicated in regulating speech are also involved in comprehending and producing sentences that have complex syntax, and yield that ability to think in abstract terms. The abstract "tools," the grave goods found with these fossils, provide corroborating evidence of these human capabilities. However, the skeletal evidence of a modern vocal tract, in itself, probably furnishes sufficient proof. The evolution of the brain is amazingly conservative. Alan Sokoloff, a biological anthropologist who studied the evolution of the brain in his Harvard University Ph.D dissertation research, found that the circuits connecting the muscles of the tongue to the neuroanatomical structures of the brainstem are almost identical in frogs and in monkeys. Therefore, given the continuity of evolution, the possibility that anatomically modern human beings 100,000 years ago could have had brains that would regulate speech, but not syntax or thought, is vanishingly small.

How Did They Get Their Brains?

Some linguists, such as Robin Burling, maintain that language really did not evolve to serve communication—that it instead developed as a vehicle of thought. The argument seems to be based on the presence of an unbridgeable gap between the emotionally triggered vocal communications of nonhuman primates and human speech. The mechanisms of Darwinian evolution supposedly cannot account for the qualitative neural distinction between the human and nonhuman brain's ability to regulate vocal communication. It is difficult to follow the reasoning behind this premise. The cognitive gap between the human and nonhuman primate brain is surely as profound as that governing vocal communication. Moreover, even larger gaps have been bridged. Mammals that nurture their infants evolved from egg-laying reptiles. And the mammalian brain differs qualitatively from the brains of reptiles.

The Darwinian mechanisms of "preadaptation," wherein an organ adapted for one purpose fortuitously is useful for a "new" function, has accounted for many of the qualitative, abrupt transitions in evolutionary history. Neural mechanisms initially adapted to regulate the precise manual motor control implicated in toolmaking could have provided the initial basis for the regulation of speech motor activity. Broca's region, though not the "seat" of language ability, is known to be involved in regulating fine manual motor control, speech production, and syntax. The studies of aphasia, Parkinson's disease, and hypoxia reviewed in the previous chapter show the linkage between speech production and syntax.

If we consider the language capabilities of the human brain in light of the present database, we can propose a reasonable evolutionary model. It assumes that the modification of neural mechanisms adapted from motor control in early hominids provided the preadaptive starting point for natural selection that yielded voluntary motor control and ultimately rule-governed syntax.[8] In a meaningful sense, learning to run away from a threatening situation, or taking advantage of an opportunity, constitutes intelligent behavior. Mutations and natural selection for rapid appropriate motor responses to environmental challenges to life or the survival of infants and children could have contributed to the enlargement of many of the neuroanatomical structures implicated in human language. Since we know that many neuroanatomical structures are implicated in both motor control and higher cognition, including language, this is a fair premise. Darwinian natural selection and preadaptation, therefore, can account for the evolution of language.

The fourfold enlargement of computational resources in parts of the human brain[9] that are active when we talk or comprehend language could in itself account for the qualitative difference between the human brain and the nonhuman primate brain. Whereas the functional distinction between a handheld calculator and a Cray supercomputer is qualitative, the morphological distinction is quantitative. The enormous memory and ultra-rapid computational speed of the supercomputer enable it to perform tasks that are qualitatively different from those possible on a calculator. Similar quantitative distinctions mark the human brain. Quantitative enlargements of prefrontal cortex, cerebellum, and basal ganglia—neuroanatomical structures implicated in regulating motor control, syntax, and thinking—differentiate the human brain from the chimpanzee brain. So far as we can tell from brain volume and the overall packaging of the brain, these changes were in place 100,000 years ago in the hominids who could talk as we do.

When and Where Did They Get Their Brains?

We do not at present have any reasonably complete skulls of the probable African ancestors of Skhul V or Jebel Qafzeh from which we could reconstruct vocal tracts. Nevertheless, the genetic data continue to indicate African ancestors who lived 150,000 to 200,000 years ago. The original studies that traced the pattern of variation of mitochondrial DNA transmitted from Eve have been reaffirmed by independent analyses of the "nuclear" DNA contributed by Adam.[10] The references to an Adam and an Eve are not simply metaphorical. Biological evolution operates on individuals. The process of natural selection involves an individual who possesses some trait coded by genes that will be transmitted to his/her children. It is most unlikely that the properties of the human brain that make speech, language, and complex thought possible were the result of one genetic variation—so there were many Adams and Eves. But at some point the brains and anatomy of our hominid ancestors were within the range of variation of present day human beings, and that is when "our" Adam and Eve lived. Most probably, they lived in Africa, but possibly in the Middle Eastern lands of the Old Testament.

The fossil record of hominid evolution and the archaeological record that were discussed in Chapter 4 suggest a time frame for the evolution of the language capabilities of the human brain. The evolution of hominid behavior can be traced in the fossil record through the "derived" anatomical features that differentiate human beings from apes. It is clear that fingers adapted for precise manual activity (Susman 1994) differentiated early hominids, who are in our line of descent, from other contemporary hominids. Therefore, one stage of the evolution of the human brain must have involved adaptations that facilitated precise manual motor control. There would not have been any reason for natural selection for fingers that facilitated precise manual motor activity in the absence of the brain mechanisms that are necessary to regulate such activity. Although chimpanzees can manipulate objects and make and use tools with their hands, they are clumsy compared with human beings. The hominid brain and hand evolved in coordinated fashion to facilitate precise manual activity. The evidence of aphasia, neurodegenerative diseases, and retardation shows that the neural bases of manual motor activity are linked to speech and syntax.

A later stage of the evolution of the brain bases of human language must have involved the elaboration of human speech. The fossil record of hominid evolution again allows us to make this inference. The anatomy involved in the production of human speech has been modified to enhance vocal communication at the expense of respiratory efficiency and protection from choking. Human beings are the only species who have a low larynx that can be obstructed with food, resulting in asphyxiation.

What Did Eve (or Adam) Talk About?

The answer to the question "What did they talk about?" might best be rephrased to "What didn't they talk about?" About every two years another study is published in some scholarly journal that purports to demonstrate that human language evolved "because" it facilitated toolmaking, hunting, warfare, courtship and mating, intergroup communication, averting aggression, sharing ideas, and so on. Some of these studies present their conclusions in charts that look like the organizational structure of a multinational corporation. A box labeled "toolmaking." A box labeled "art." Boxes everywhere, with lines connecting the boxes to show how communication facilitates the activity represented in each box. The diagrams quickly look like cocoons as the language lines proliferate. But it is safe to assume that *any* human activity is enhanced by the ability to communicate information—concrete, abstract, or emotional—conveyed by language. There is no reason to believe that Eve or Adam found language less useful or behaved differently. They talked about everything and everyone that concerned them.

Morality—Good and Evil

It is appropriate to return at this point to the main premise of Noam Chomsky's theories. His basic claim, that the central aspects

of human language are determined by an innate, genetically transmitted "organ" of the brain, has had an impact far beyond the
bounds of linguistic research.[11] As we noted earlier, Chomsky and
many linguists believe that the linguistic environment in essence
simply activates rules of grammar that are present in the child's
innate universal grammar. Chomsky is not alone in proposing that
a gene or genes determine a complex, key aspect of human nature.
In his book *The Moral Animal*, Robert Wright misinterprets recent
work in evolutionary biology and proposes the existence of a
morality gene. The theory that he develops resembles the Chomskian linguistic model. His model must, like Chomsky's, claim that
the brain's "moral organ" is qualitatively similar for all human
beings.[12] However, if human morality actually were regulated by a
genetically specified organ, then, given the universal presence of
genetic variation, many individuals, their children, their children's
children, entire families, and communities would inherently and
irredeemably be immoral This would present a moral dilemma;
would it be necessary, for the public good, to identify and isolate
these immoral-gene carriers?[13]

However, like the Chomskian proposal for a language gene
governing universal grammar, the claim for a morality gene is false.
Although some of the basic qualities that enter into human moral
behavior, such as compassion for closely related individuals, may
have a genetic, Darwinian basis, "higher" human morality is not in
our genes. Morality clearly has a cognitive-linguistic cultural basis.
One unfortunate consequence of this more subtle basis for human
morality is its Manichaean cast—it can yield behavior both for
good and for evil that transcends the capacity of any other animal.

The cognitive basis of this higher human morality is simple. We
can place ourselves in the position of the "other" and through the
medium of language convince others. Chimpanzees, the closest link
that we have to our common hominid-ape ancestor, clearly lack
this ability. Jane Goodall's detailed descriptions of chimpanzees eating their prey after a successful hunt are chilling. Chimpanzees
calmly chew away on living monkeys, passing tidbits to one another as the victim screams. Goodall has documented horrific episodes

that went on for forty minutes, until the victim finally died. No human hunters would act in this manner unless they were depraved and intended to inflict pain. Our moral judgment, that an individual who would act in this manner is "depraved," derives from our being able to place ourselves in the position of the other.

Wright and other sociobiologists often invoke gene selection theories to explain the biological bases of morality. According to these theories, it is advantageous to exterminate competitors so long as you preserve creatures that carry a certain proportion of your genes. Gene selection theories are also clearly irrelevant to human moral behavior. Moreover, they are pernicious, dangerous tools in the hands of demagogues. As we noted in earlier chapters, language tends to isolate those of a gene pool. The expedient adopted by the Nazi occupiers of Europe during World War II—of murdering innocent French, Greek, Russian, and Serbian civilians when partisans shot German soldiers in combat—would be justified by a pseudo-Darwinian moral code that justified any action that preserved "similar" genes. If human morality were based on gene selection theories, the murder of six million Jews in the Holocaust, or one million Armenians in World War I, or 500,000 Tutsi in 1994 would also be justified.

Humans who are capable of placing themselves in the position of the other can act in a truly altruistic manner—that is, act in behalf of another person or living creature without preserving their genes, without the expectation of any reward or future benefit. The labored tit-for-tat scenarios devised by evolutionary psychologists are irrelevant. Altruism expects no material reward. Perversely, humans placing themselves in the position of the other can act to inflict pain and hurt beyond the capacity of any other species. The systematic rapes of the Yugoslavian "civil" war that were documented in 1994 were beyond the cognitive power of any ape. We can do good or evil, and the basis is cognitive-linguistic.

The historical record demonstrates the cognitive-linguistic basis of human morality. The thirteenth-century Mongol armies of Jenghiz Khan swept across Asia. Mongol military superiority was based on horsemen who could attack and retreat, loosing a storm of arrows as they rode, and on ruthless terror. The Mongols were masters at placing themselves in the position of their adversaries and doing whatever was necessary to terrify people into surrendering.

Two examples will suffice. The ancient city of Merv capitulated in February 1221. As the historian René Grousett notes in his classic work *The Empire of the Steppes: A History of Central Asia*, "Tolui, the son of Jenghiz seated on a golden chair in the plain of Merv, witnessed the mass execution. Men, women, and children were separated, distributed in herds among the various battalions, and beheaded" (Grousett, 1970, 240). Mongol siege tactics used captives as human shields. "To capture a city the Mongols would round up the male population of the surrounding districts—from the countryside and open towns—and drive it at the point of the sword against ditch and wall. What if these wretches were mown down by their fellow countrymen, so long as their bodies filled the ditch and their repeated attacks exhausted the garrison" (p. 242).

But Mongol "morals" clearly had nothing to do with Mongol genes. Kublai Khan, the grandson of Jenghiz Khan, who ascended the Mongol throne on June 4, 1260, was hailed as a "qutuqtu," a venerable divine, by Buddhist sages. Kublai Khan had sent for the Tibetan Sakya-Pa lama Phags-Pa, who in 1258 convinced Kublai of the virtues of Buddhism. The Sakya-Pa order of monks then converted the Mongols to Tibetan Buddhism. The tenets of Buddhism include compassion to all living creatures. The logic of Tibetan Lamaism states the following: (1) Everyone owes devotion to his/her mother. (2) Earthly existence is a series of endless reincarnations over endless time. (3) Therefore, every creature is, or was, your mother, to whom you owe devotion. (4) So you must regard and honor all living creatures as your mother. (5) If you act otherwise, you will suffer in your next reincarnation.

Kublai Khan, whose court Marco Polo visited, founded monasteries, repaired the imperial roads, planted shade trees, and provided assistance for old scholars, orphans, and the sick and infirm. Buddhist influence was so strong that rice and millet were distributed to poor families. Marco Polo's journals note that Kublai Khan himself fed thirty thousand paupers daily.

That brings us back to the question of what Eve may have said to Adam, and he to her. Eve and Adam surely did not discourse on the nature of good and evil. Nor did they discuss the nature of language or quantum mechanics. But it is probable that the things they talked about were the concerns of our very immediate pre-industrial, pre-agricultural ancestors. Food, weather, anger, affection, tools, and the nature of the world as they could best explain it. These traditions survive, though attenuated by agriculture and the inserted artifacts of the industrialized world. Shamans still drum and dance throughout much of the world to placate or drive out evil spirits. Morality is a product of human culture that developed over a period of at least 100,000 years. The major religions of the world that codify higher morality are barely 5,000 years old.

Coda

In the beginning there was the word.

And then over time our ancestors gradually evolved the capability for speech, for ever more words, and for complex thought. With the final Eve came the gift of speaking and thinking as we do. And that gift allowed us to populate the world, displacing other hominids and many other species. Speech appears to be one of the key elements, if not *the* key element, in fully developed human language and cognition. By speaking to one another, we have shaped and transmitted human culture and achieved great civilizations. Writing, which ultimately codes speech, is itself a product of human language and cognitive ability. Even now, fingering the computer keyboard before me, I find it difficult, if not impossible, to form these thoughts without the unspoken sounds of the words that fall into place in my mind.

But the time of Eve is long past, in terms both of human life and of human culture. And the question that currently faces us is, What use will we make of speech and language? Evolution in itself has no direction. The old creation myths will not suffice. We are not the lords of creation, made in God's image because we talk, masters of the birds and beasts, which cannot speak. The purpose to human life is surely that we must use the gift of speech, language, and thought to act to enhance life and love, to vanquish needless suffering and murderous violence—to achieve a yet higher morality. For if we do not, Eve's descendants will reach their end, marking another brief, failed "experiment" in the long evolutionary history of our planet.

And no other creature will be here to sing a dirge or tell the story of our passing, for we alone can talk.

Notes

1. The detailed results are reported in our 1995 paper in *Aviation, Space and Environmental Medicine*.

2. The multiregional theory advanced by Milford Wolpoff is presented in the paper by Frayer et al. (1993). Specific claims that Neanderthals' speech ability wasn't different from ours are presented in many papers, e.g., Arensburg et al. (1990), Houghton (1993), and Falk (1975). These issues and a reappraisal of the speech capabilities of the Neanderthals will be discussed in detail in the chapters that follow.

3. Some readers may recall that Owen Lattimore, one of the most knowledgeable American experts on China, was charged with "losing" China in the infamous congressional witch-hunts of the 1950s.

4. The Haskins Laboratories research group's research paper, (Liberman et al. 1967) that described this process marks a milestone in our understanding of the special nature of human linguistic ability.

5. Sheila Blumstein and Kenneth Stevens showed that human listeners will "hear" the consonant and vowel of a syllable such as [da] even when only the first 5/1000 of a second of the speech signal is available. Human beings appear to learn to recognize the syllables of their native language starting almost from birth, perhaps before birth, since they can hear and recognize their mother's voice in the last month of fetal life.

6. Many of the details are in my 1984 book, *The Biology and Evolution of Language.*

7. Many animals have specialized auditory systems that allow them to keep track of sounds that occur much closer in time. Bats, for example, can keep track of microsecond differences by means of a specialized sonar-like system that lets them track objects in total darkness.

CHAPTER 2

1. McGrew's 1993 paper is a concise summary of many chimpanzee field observation projects.

2. The stone tools that Kanzi copied resembled the "Oldowan" tools associated with fossil hominids that lived about two million years ago. The place of Oldowan tools in archaelogical record is discussed in Chapter 4.

3. The noted psychologist David Premack, who pioneered the study of language and cognition in chimpanzees, at one time proposed that pedagogy was *the* characteristic that differentiated human beings from chimpanzees.

4. Though some linguists claim otherwise, mental retardation affects language. Clemens Benda noted this in his classic book on Down's syndrome.

5. The paper was presented at a conference at the University of Bielefeld, in Germany, in 1992.

6. One question that must occur to you is, "How do talking birds talk?" The answer is that they don't really "talk." Birds produce sound by a very different mechanism. They have two "syringes," devices that produce almost "pure" tones (sinusoidal waves). Crawford Greenewalt's definitive study of birdsong showed that talking birds mimic speech by placing a sinusoid at each of the two lowest formant frequencies of the speech signal that they're mimicing. The bird also interrupts the syringeal output at the speech pitch rate. Perceptual experiments performed by Robert Remez and his colleague show that if you put yourself into the right mental set, the bird mimicry will "sound" like speech. Bird speech mimicry otherwise doesn't sound like speech. Greenewalt, incidentally, wasn't a "certified," Ph.D. -holding "researcher." He carried out his research while also directing the operations of the DuPont chemical corporation.

CHAPTER 3

1. Many otherwise informed scholars didn't realize until many years after Crelin's book was published that normal human adults don't look like newborn infants. Stephen Jay Gould, for example, in a lengthy book published in 1977 defended the theory of "neoteny," which holds that the rapid evolution of human

beings stems from our retaining the characteristics of newborn infants. But, in fact, the only human adults who retain some of the features of newborn infants are the victims of Down's syndrome, in which genetic anomalies result in retarded mental and physical development. Clemens Benda's 1969 book showed that many of the anatomical signs of the syndrome actually were typical features of healthy, normal newborn infants.

2. The occurrence of sudden infant death syndrome (SIDS) at about the age of three months may reflect inappropriate changes in the neural control of respiration in infants that normally occurs at this age. Mouth breathing becomes possible as the larynx begins to descend.

3. The fact that human beings and other mammals have a very different anatomical arrangement for breathing and swallowing was known to Charles Darwin before the publication of *On the Origin of Species* in 1859. Since Darwin himself did not carry out a series of anatomical dissections, anatomists must have been aware of this distinction in the early years of the nineteenth century. In the twentieth century, in a career that spanned the two world wars, the British anatomist Victor Negus systematically studied the larynges and airways of different species. Negus established the fact that adult human beings have a unique anatomical arrangement for breathing and swallowing. Although his last book was published in 1949, he missed the true significance of the human SVT's role in speech production. This, of course, doesn't discredit Negus's achievements, since the modern period of intensive research on speech physiology didn't really start until the 1950s except for the groundbreaking study by the Japanese scholars Tsutomo Chiba and Masato Kajiyama, which they published in English in Tokyo in 1941 when Japan attacked the United States. The book's distribution was suppressed by the Japanese military. Chiba managed to bury a copy in his garden, and it was republished in 1958.

4. Howells also concludes that Neanderthals cannot be considered to be variant humans; their skulls are simply outside the possible range of variation of human skulls.

5. Karen Landahl, the Brown University graduate student whose study of the development of language in children was discussed earlier, is at present a professor at the University of Chicago.

6. Like most scientific projects, this work was a group effort. Dennis Klatt was an accomplished speech scientist at the Research Laboratory for Electronics at MIT (his untimely death cut short a series of superb studies of speech production and perception). William Wilson, an M.D., studied primate behavior in the Department of Psychology at the University of Connecticut. Katherine S. Harris has made substantial contributions to our knowledge of speech production and has trained many speech scientists at Haskins Laboratories and the Graduate Center of the City University of New York. We all depended on each other's special knowledge.

CHAPTER 4

1. A concise discussion of the genetic evidence and genetics is presented in *The Cambridge Encyclopedia of Human Evolution*, ed. S. Jones, R. Martin, and D. Pilbeam (Cambridge: Cambridge University Press, 1992), 225–321.

2. Bernard Wood's 1992 account of the evolution of australopithecines presents the evidence gathered to that date in a reasoned manner.

3. Chris Stringer's concise discussion (1992) of this period of hominid evolution will be useful to readers who want to follow the continuing debate on our evolution. Stringer's views are not "balanced." He is an exponent of the "Out of Africa," or "Eve," hypothesis, but that is, as I hope you will agree, the correct theory concerning the evolution of modern human beings.

4. Other late (about 34,000 years ago) Neanderthal sites show similar signs of cultural borrowing between the last Neanderthals and the first modern humans in Europe (Hublin et al. 1996).

5. Manual sign language, though it can serve as an alternative channel of communication for modern hearing-deprived human beings who have modern human brains, inherently limits this capability. Manual sign language runs counter to the irreversible trend among hominids toward the pervasive use of ever more complex tools. Manual gestures continue to supplement vocal communication. David MacNeill, who works at the University of Chicago, has convincingly shown that manual gestures supplement speech. Practically all of us wave our hands to indicate movement, emphasize words, signal the ends of sentences, and so on. It makes our meaning clearer, but we don't have to do this. Gestural communication probably played a larger role in the early stages of hominid evolution, but it never was the exclusive medium of language.

6. See Stringer's survey article (1992).

7. One recent attempt to reconstruct the La Chapelle-aux-Saints Neanderthal fossil with a modern human vocal tract in which the mouth and pharynx were of equal length provided the Neanderthal with an exceedingly small tongue (Houghton 1993). However, this again is an impossible solution; the small tongue would not have allowed the Neanderthal to swallow food.

8. The reconstruction of the La Chapelle-aux-Saints Neanderthal skull used here is that prepared between 1911 and 1913 by Marcellin Boule at the Musée de l'Homme in Paris. The more recent reconstruction by Jean-Louis Heim doesn't change the basicranial distance between the spinal column and the back of the roof of the mouth that is the skeletal mark of a long mouth and a nonhuman vocal tract.

9. I find it both gratifying and amazing that my son Daniel, who first saw a Neanderthal skull when he was six years old, is carrying out this complex project. The basis for this new Neanderthal vocal tract reconstruction will form part of his forthcoming book, *The Human Skull*.

10. This basic fact makes irrelevant the argument of Arensburg et al. (1990) that Neanderthals had a human vocal tract. Baruch Arensburg and his colleagues,

noting similarities between the shape of the Kebara Neanderthal fossil hyoid bone and human hyoid bones, claimed that the Neanderthal hyoid and larynx must have occupied the low position encountered in adult humans. However, their claim is based on the assertion that the human larynx and the hyoid bone (a bone that supports the larynx) retain a fixed position with respect to the cervical vertebrae and skull from birth on. This is false. All known anatomical data show that the human hyoid bone and larynx do not maintain a fixed position throughout life; they descend from a high, apelike position in the human neonate to a low position in normal adults. Moreover, the human hyoid bone's shape doesn't change as it and the larynx descend. Therefore, the shape of the Kebara hyoid won't tell us where the Kebara Neanderthal's larynx was positioned (Lieberman 1994).

11. This effect is apparent in the data of some of the earliest quantitative studies of the physiology of human speech—by Gunnar Fant, of the Royal Institute of Technology in Stockholm, in 1960, and by Kenneth Stevens and Arthur House, at MIT, in 1955. It was explicitly noted by Kenneth Stevens in 1972. The details are discussed in my 1984 book.

CHAPTER 5

1. Paul MacLean's comparative studies of the evolution of the brain link the evolution of mammals to the "motor cortex." The anterior portion of this neuroanatomical structure, the cingulate gyrus, regulates the vocalizations that young mammals use to keep in touch with their mothers as well as maternal behavior (as demonstrated, for example, in Slotnick 1967). The cingulate gyrus also plays a part in the regulation of human speech, motor control, emotion, and cognition through neural "circuits" that connect it to other parts of the brain.

2. Norman Geschwind's (1970) theory exemplifies the model presented in most current linguistic theories. Geschwind proposed that the neurological basis of human language was a "circuit" consisting of Wernicke's and Broca's areas linked by the arcuate fasciculus (a cortical pathway). Wernicke's area essentially processed incoming speech signals in this model; information was then transmitted to Broca's area, which served as the "expressive" language output device. It is probable that Geschwind himself would have modified this model, had he not died before the experimental data discussed in this chapter became available; his close associates M-Marcel Mesulam and Frank Benson played central roles in the development of the circuit model of the brain.

3. Note the papers of Metter and his associates.

4. Patricia Goldman-Rakic has been studying prefrontal cortical activity in primates and humans for many years. Her 1987 paper is a useful summary of her findings.

5. The 1987 paper by Mark Bear and his associates is an example of research on the physiological mechanisms that modify synapses.

6. André Parent's 1986 book reviews many of these studies. He discusses the evolution and nature of subcortical basal ganglia circuitry as revealed by tracer studies and other techniques.

7. Although our present knowledge of the brain is still fragmentary, evidence from converging studies indicates that the human brain has a "functional language system." The probable nature and evolution of this system is discussed in my forthcoming book, *The Functional Language System of the Human Brain*.

8. The debate between the views expressed by Noam Chomsky and his adherents—for example, Jerry Fodor, Steven Pinker, and Ray Jackendoff—and the view expressed here (and by many other students of language and the brain, such as Elizabeth Bates, Andrew Meltzoff, and Anthony Tomasello) centers on whether an innate, genetically specified module transmits the details of grammar for human language.

9. Lee Lisker and Arthur Abramson in their 1964 acoustic study examined actual speech samples from native speakers of languages that were representative of many of the world's language "groups." They found that "voice onset time" (VOT), the timing between the start of phonation and the moment that the vocal tract was opened, was used to differentiate words in all of these languages. Subsequent studies have extended the database and, with minor changes, support their original findings. In short, Johannes Müller's theory was reaffirmed by means of electronic instruments that he didn't even dream of two hundred years ago.

10. Shari Baum and her colleagues replicated the effect in a study that also correlated aphasic symptoms with CT scans. Other recent CT studies show that aphasia can occur with subcortical damage, without damage to the neocortex (e.g., Mega and Alexander 1994).

11. Ross Cunnington and the research group directed by John Bradshaw in Australia have shown that a basal ganglia circuit to the supplementary motor area of the cortex is implicated in regulating manual timing. The ability of Parkinson's patients to maintain control of time intervals when they have to push a sequence of buttons with their fingers also deteriorates.

12. The elegant study by Lange et al. (1992) tested Parkinson's patients on and off their medications, by means of a battery of computer-implemented cognitive tests.

13. Similar results have been reported by Grossman's group at the University of Pennsylvania for English-speaking subjects and by Natsopoulos for Greek-speaking subjects.

14. Arend Bouhuy's 1974 book, *Breathing*, provides an accurate account of respiratory physiology that can be followed without an extensive technical background.

15. The experimental procedures and results are reported in a short paper published in the journal *Nature* in 1994 and in a more detailed account in *Aviation, Space and Environmental Medicine*.

16. A reader's comprehension would obviously be facilitated if she or he also

knew that the word *dog* could refer to a device that is used to bolt a ship's bulkhead, but most readers would realize after reading the sentence that Albert was not abusing an animal.

17. Just and Carpenter (1992) present a comprehensive review of recent studies concerning verbal working memory and data showing that one cannot comprehend syntax without taking into account the possible meanings of each word of a sentence. Their study refutes linguistic theories that claim that syntax processing takes place in a "module" structurally isolated from a "lexical" (dictionary) module. A number of clever experiments inspired by Elizabeth Bates, who studies language development in a neurolinguistic context at the University of California at San Diego (Bates et al. 1995; Blackwell and Bates 1995; and MacDonald et al. 1994), show that human beings take simultaneous account of lexical, probabilistic, and semantic information coded in the brain's dictionary in order to comprehend the meaning of speech or written texts. The process is not carried out in a series of modules that conform to the architecture of conventional digital computers.

18. Many other phenomena indicate the central role that speech plays in language processing. The role of speech sounds in the brain's dictionary is evident in the 1996 paper of Hannah and Antonio Damasio and their colleagues at the University of Iowa College of Medicine. The Damasios are central players in current neurophysiological research. Their parallel PET studies of neurologically intact subjects and patients with brain damage show that the brain's dictionary couples visual and motor cortex areas that code the concepts of a word to areas of the cortex in which the sounds that convey a word are parceled out in semantic categories such as tools, people, and animals. The "motor theory of speech perception," developed by Alvin Liberman and his colleagues at Haskins Laboratories (Liberman et al. 1967; Liberman and Mattingly 1985), proposes that the neural mechanisms involved in speech production subvocally model the incoming acoustic signal. According to this theory, people interpret speech sounds in terms of the articulatory gestures that underlie the production of speech. This accounts for otherwise inexplicable effects like that noted by Harry McGurk. If you simultaneously look at a motion picture of a person saying the sound [ba] and listen to the sound [ga], you will "hear" the intermediate [da]. The explanation rests on certain consonants' being highly valued because of their articulatory and acoustic properties (Stevens 1972). The English consonantal series allows only [ba], [da], and [ga]. When visual articulatory [ba] and acoustic [ga] cues conflict, we hear the intermediate [da].

19. The experiments of Hata and Stryker (1994) and Rauschecker and Korte (1993) show these effects. Gerald Edelman discusses the general process in his book *Neural Darwinism*.

20. The FMRI study was reported by Thomas Elbert and his colleagues in the journal *Science* in October 1995.

21. The development of speech and syntax in children has been studied

intensively for decades. The renowned linguist Roman Jakobson pointed out that the structure of language might be revealed by the stages in which children acquired the concepts governing speech, word structure, and syntax. A collection of Jakobson's essays, *On Language*, was published in 1990. Some of the details concerning the acquisition of speech by children are noted in my 1984 book, *The Biology and Evolution of Language*. Lois Bloom and Roger Brown wrote classic books on the acquisition of syntax by English-speaking children that are accurate and readable.

22. MIT's alumni magazine, *Technology Review*, for example, announced in 1990 a major project that would make use of Chomsky's most recent research to implement a language translating system, but no progress on the project was subsequently reported.

23. James Anderson's recent book on associative neural networks is a good introduction to current work. Paul Churchland's books on this topic present similar material in a philosophical context.

24. Chomskian linguists somehow fail to address the question of how children learn to produce or comprehend the sentences that constitute the vast "peripheral" grammar. If general "learning" can account for how children learn this part of the grammar, which specialists on child language research as Dan Slobin of the University of California estimate covers at least 95 percent of the grammar, then why is innate knowledge necessary for the remaining 5 percent of "core" grammar?

25. The implications of the Saffran et al. study (1996) are discussed in the same issue of *Science* by Elizabeth Bates and Jeffrey Elman of the University of California at San Diego. Bates and Elman note that the demonstrated power of associative learning of human infants in this linguistic task obviates the need for a Chomskian innate language organ that specifies the details of syntax.

CHAPTER 6

1. The acoustic correlates of speech were noted in Chapter 2. The helicopter study is part of a project aimed at developing techniques to aid investigations of aircraft accidents (Protopappas and Lieberman, in press).

2. These effects were noted for one three-month-old infant in Lieberman (1984). Patricia Kuhl has shown that by the age of six months virtually all infants can do this. It's interesting that computer systems designed to recognize speech still cannot perform this operation as well as infants can.

3. The research was performed at the University of Connecticut, and the children were all monolingual natives of eastern Connecticut.

4. Research reported by Marc Hauser at Harvard University suggests that monkeys can in certain circumstances produce "deceptive" food calls.

5. As was noted in earlier chapters, some theories for the evolution of lan-

guage claim that manual signs rather than speech were used by the early hominid species that lived between 5 million and 500,000 years ago (Hewes 1973). However, this is unlikely even for these archaic hominid species, for the reasons noted in Chapter 4. It is even less likely that manual sign language was the exclusive means of linguistic communication 100,000 years ago in anatomically modern human hominids who had modern vocal tracts.

6. The "movement" involves differential bone growth from infancy to adulthood and is part of a complex process that differentiates the human skull from those of other animals and extinct hominids, including *Homo erectus* and the classic Neanderthals. Daniel Lieberman's book *The Human Skull* (in press) covers these issues in detail.

7. A typical study is that of Manley and Braley (1950).

8. Doreen Kimura (1979) independently proposed a similar preadaptive basis for the brain mechanisms that regulate human speech motor control.

9. The comparative studies of Stephan and his colleagues (1981), mentioned in Chapter 5, document increases in the volume of the neuroanatomical structures implicated in both adaptive motor control and language.

10. See Chris Stringer's review articles.

11. Ray Jackendoff's 1994 book presents some of the arguments for innate "organs" of the brain that supposedly govern other aspects of human cognition.

12. Some of the arguments for genetic uniformity in humans proposed by exponents of "genes" for grammar and morality are amusing. For example, Steven Pinker, who supports Chomsky's views, argues that sexual reproduction would result in unviable progeny if the range of human genetic variation were great. For example, the parts of the heart specified by a mother and a father would not "match," and the embryo would die. Pinker appears to believe that sexual activity at the appropriate time of the month always results in the production of progeny. However, Pinker's biology is wrong; 50 to 75 percent of all human embryos are spontaneously aborted (Roberts and Lowe 1975). The actual reproductive data thus refute his argument and do not support the Chomskian claim that a language gene produces an identical universal grammar in all "normal" human beings.

13. It is not difficult to imagine how eugenic planners might carry out a program that would eliminate the "abnormal" carriers of "defective" morality genes. Recent events show what happens when supposedly rational people believe that other people are genetically inferior.

References

Alexander, G. E., M. R. Delong, and P. L. Strick. 1986. Parallel organization of segregated circuits linking basal ganglia and cortex. *Annual Review of Neuroscience* 9:357–81.

Alexander, M. P., M. A. Naeser, and C. L. Palumbo. 1987. Correlations of subcortical CT lesion sites and aphasia profiles. *Brain* 110:961–91.

Arensburg, B., L. A. Schepartz, A. M. Tillier, B. Vandermeersch, and Y. Rak. 1990. A reappraisal of the anatomical basis for speech in Middle Palaeolithic hominids. *American Journal of Physical Anthropology* 83:137–46.

Baddeley, A. D. 1986. *Working memory.* Oxford: Clarendon Press.

Barbujani, G., and R. R. Sokal. 1990. Zones of sharp genetic change in Europe are also linguistic boundaries. *Proceedings of the National Academy of Science, USA* 187:1816–19.

———. 1991. Genetic population structure of Italy. II: Physical and cultural barriers to gene flow. *American Journal of Human Genetics* 48:398–411.

Bates, E., C. Harris, V. Marchman, B. Wulfeck, and M. Kritchevsky. 1995. Production of complex syntax in normal aging and Alzheimer's disease. *Language and Cognitive Processes* 10:487–539.

Bauer, R. H. 1993. Lateralization of neural control for vocalization by the frog (Rana pipiens). *Psychobiology* 21:243–48.

Baum, S. R., S. E. Blumstein, M. A. Naeser, and C. L. Palumbo. 1990. Temporal dimensions of consonant and vowel production: An acoustic and CT scan analysis of aphasic speech. *Brain and Language* 39:33–56.

Bear, M. F., L. N. Cooper, and F. F. Ebner. 1987. A physiological basis for a theory of synaptic modification. *Science* 237:42–48.

Benda, C. E. 1969 *Down's syndrome: Mongolism and its management.* New York: Grune and Stratton.

Bergland, O. 1963. *The bony nasopharynx: A roentgen-craniometric study. Acta Otodontologia Scandinavica* (Oslo) 21, sippl. 35.

Blackwell, A., and E. Bates. 1995. Inducing agrammatic profiles in normals: Evidence for the selective vulnerability of morphology under cognitive resource limitation. *Journal of Cognitive Neuroscience* 7:28–257.

Bloom, L. 1973. *One word at a time: The use of single word utterances before syntax.* The Hague: Mouton.

Blumstein, S. E., W. E. Cooper, H. Goodglass, S. Statlender, and J. Gottlieb. 1980. Production deficits in apahasia: A voice-onset time analysis. *Brain and Language* 9:153–70.

Blumstein, S. E., and K. N. Stevens. 1980. Perceptual invariance and onset spectra for stop consonants in different vowel environments. *Journal of the Acoustical Society of America* 67:648–62.

Boesch, C., and H. Boesch. 1993. Aspects of transmission of tool-use in wild chimpanzees. In *Tools, language and cognition in human evolution,* ed. K. R. Gibson and T. Ingold, 171–84. Cambridge: Cambridge University Press.

Bond, Z. S. 1976. Identification of vowels excerpted from neutral nasal contexts. *Journal of the Acoustical Society of America* 59:1229–32.

Bosma, J. F. 1975. Anatomic and physiologic development of the speech apparatus. In *Human communication and its disorders,* ed. D. B. Towers, 469–81. New York: Raven.

Boule, M. 1911–13. L'homme fossile de la Chapelle-aux-Saints. *Annales Paléontologie* 6:109; 7:21, 85; 8:1.

Bouhuys, A. 1974. *Breathing.* New York: Grune and Stratton.

Broca, P. 1861. Remarques sur le siège de la faculté de la parole y articulée, suivies d'une observation d' aphemie (perte de parole). *Bulletin de la Société d'Anatomie* (Paris) 36:330–57.

Brodmann, K. 1912. Ergebnisse über die vergleichende histologishe Lokalisation der Grosshirnrinde mit besonderer Berücksichtigung des Stirnhirns. *Anatomischer Anzeiger (Supplement)* 41:157–216.

Brown, R. W. 1973. *A first language.* Cambridge: Harvard University Press.

Buhr, R. D. 1980. The emergence of vowels in an infant. *Journal of Speech and Hearing Research* 23:75–94.

Cahill, D. R., M. J. Orland, and C. C. Reading. 1990. *Atlas of human cross-sectional anatomy with CT and MR images.* 2nd ed. New York: Wiley-Liss.

Carré, R., B. Lindblom, and P. MacNeilage. 1994. Acoustic factors in the evolution of the human vocal tract. *Journal of the Acoustical Society of America* 95:2924.

Cheney, D. L., and R. M. Seyfarth. 1990. *How monkeys see the world: Inside the mind of another species.* Chicago: University of Chicago Press.

Chiba, T., and J Kajiyama. 1941. *The vowel: Its nature and structure.* Tokyo: Tokyo-Kaisekan Publishing.

Chomsky, N. 1986. *Knowledge of language: Its nature, origin and use.* New York: Prager.

Churchland, P. M. 1995. *The engine of reason, the seat of the soul: A philosophical joruney into the brain.* Cambridge: MIT Press.

Crelin, E. S. 1969. *Anatomy of the newborn: An atlas.* Philadelphia: Lea and Febiger.

Croft, W. 1991. *Syntactic categories and grammatical relations.* Chicago: University of Chicago Press.

Cummings, J. L. 1993. Frontal-subcortical circuits and human behavior. *Archives of Neurology* 50:873–80.

Cunnington, R., R. Iansek, J. L. Bradshaw, and J. G. Philips. 1995. Movement-related potentials in Parkinson's disease: Presence and predictability of temporal and spatial cues. *Brain* 118:935–50.

Curtiss, S. 1977. *Genie: A psycholinguistic study of a modern-day "Wild Child."* New York: Academic Press.

Damasio, H., T. J. Grabowski, D. Tranel, R. D. Hichwa, and A. R. Damasio. 1996. A neural basis for lexical retrieval. *Nature* 380:409–505.

Darwin, C. 1859. *On the origin of species.* Facsimile ed. 1964. Cambridge: Harvard University Press.

Davidson. I. 1991. The archaeology of language origins: A review. *Antiquity* 65:39–48.

Delong, M. R., A. P. Georgopoulos, and M. D. Crutcher. 1983. Corticobasal ganglia relations and coding of motor performance. In *Neural coding of motor performance: Experimental brain research.* Supplement 7, ed. J. Massion, J. Paillard, W. Schultz, and M. Wiesendanger, 30–40. Berlin: Springer.

Denenberg, V. H. 1981. Hemispheric laterality in animals and the effects of early experience. *Behavioral and Brain Sciences* 4:1–49.

Donald, M. 1991. *Origins of the modern mind.* Cambridge: Harvard University Press.

Edelman, G. M. 1987. *Neural Darwinism.* New York: Basic Books.

Eimas, P. D. 1974. Auditory and linguistic processing of cues for place of articulation by infants. *Perception and Psychophysics* 16:513–21.

Engen, E., and T. Engen, 1983. *Rhode Island test of language structure.* Baltimore: University Park Press.

Falk, D. 1975. Comparative anatomy of the larynx in man and the chimpanzee: Implications for language in Neanderthal. *American Journal of Physical Anthropology* 43:123–32.

Fant, G. 1960. *Acoustic theory of speech production.* The Hague: Mouton.

Fitch, W. T. III, 1993. Vocal tract length and the evolution of language. Ph. D. diss. Brown University.

Fodor, J. 1983. *Modularity of mind*. Cambridge: MIT Press.

Frayer, D. W., M. H. Wolpoff, A. G. Thorne, F. H. Smith, and G. G. Pope. 1993. Theories of modern human origins: The paleontological test. *American Anthropologist* 95:14–50.

Gardner, B. T., and R. A. Gardner. In press. Development of phrases in the utterances of children and cross-fostered chimpanzees. In *The Ethological Roots of Culture*, ed. R. A. Gardner, B. T. Gardner, B. Chiarelli, and R. Plooj. Dordrecht: Kluwer Academic Publishers.

Gardner, R. A., and B. T. Gardner. 1971. Two-way communication with an infant chimpanzee. In *Behavior of nonhuman primates*, ed. A. Schrier and F. Stollnitz, vol 4. New York: Academic Press.

Gardner, R. A., and B. T. Gardner. 1984. A vocabulary test for chimpanzees (*Pan troglodytes*). *Journal of Comparative Psychology* 4:381–404.

Gardner, R. A., B. T. Gardner, and T. E. Van Cantfort. 1989. *Teaching sign language to chimpanzees*. Albany: State University of New York Press.

George, S. L. 1978. A longitudinal and cross-sectional analysis of the growth of the postnatal cranial base angle. *American Journal of Physical Anthropology* 49:171–78.

Geschwind, N. 1970. The organization of language and the brain. *Science* 170:940–44.

Goldin-Meadow, S. 1993. When does gesture become language? A study of gesture used as the primary communication by deaf children of hearing parents. In *Tools, language and cognition in human evolution,* ed. K. R. Gibson and T. Ingold, 63–85. Cambridge: Cambridge University Press.

Goldman-Rakic, P. S. 1987. Circuitry of primate prefrontal cortex and regulation of behavior by representational memory. In *Handbook of physiology*. Sec 1., *The nervous system*. Vol. 5, *Higher functions of the brain*, ed. F. Plum and V. Mountcastle 373–417. Bethesda, Md.: American Physiological Society.

Goldstein, K. 1948. *Language and language disturbances*. New York: Grune and Stratton.

Goodall, J. 1986. *The chimpanzees of Gombe: Patterns of behavior*. Cambridge: Harvard University Press.

Gopnik M. 1990. Feature-blind grammar and dysphasia. *Nature* 344:715.

Gopnik M., and M. Crago. 1991. Familial segregation of a developmental language disorder. *Cognition*. 39:1–50.

Gottlieb, G. 1975. Development of species identification in ducklings: I. Nature of perceptual deficits caused by embryonic auditory deprivation. *Journal of Comparative and Physiological Psychology* 89:387–89

Greenewalt, C. H. 1968. *Bird song: Acoustics and physiology*. Washington, D.C.: Smithsonian Institution Press.

Grosmangin, C. 1979. *Base du crane et pharynx dans leur rapports avec l'appareil de langage articulé*. Mémoires du Laboratoire d'Anatomie de la Faculté de Medicine de Paris, no. 40-1979.

Gross, C. 1995. The representation of space in the brain. Lecture at Brown University, January 26.

Gross, M. 1979. On the failure of generative grammar. *Language* 55:859-85.

Grossman, M., S. Carvell, S. Gollomp, M. B. Stern, M. Reivich, D. Morrison, A. Alavi, and H. I. Hurtig, 1993. Cognitive and physiological substrates of impaired sentence processing in Parkinson's disease. *Journal of Cognitive Neuroscience* 5:480–98.

Grossman, M., S. Carvell, S. Gollomp, M. B. Stern, G. Vernon, and H. I. Hurtig. 1991. Sentence comprehension and praxis deficits in Parkinson's disease. *Neurology* 41:1620–28.

Grousset, R. 1970. *The empire of the steppes: A history of Central Asia*. Translated by Naomi Walford. New Brunswick, N.J.: Rutgers University Press.

Hamilton, W. D. 1964. The genetical evolution of social behavior, pts. 1, 2. *Journal of Theoretical Biology* 7:1–52.

Harnad, S. 1995. Review of Paul Churchland, *The engine of reason, the seat of the soul: A philosophical journey into the brain*. *Nature* 378:455.

Hata, Y., and M. P. Stryker. 1994. Control of thalamocortical afferent rearrangement by postsynaptic activity in developing visual cortex. *Science* 263:1732–35.

Hauser, M. D., C. S. Evans, and P. Marler. 1993. The role of articulation in the production of rhesus monkey (Macaca mulatta) vocalizations. *Animal Behavior* 45: 423–33.

Hayes, K. J., and C. Hayes. 1951. The intellectual development of a home-raised chimpanzee. *Proceedings of the American Philosophical Society* 95:105–9.

Heim, J. L. 1974. Les hommes fossiles de La Ferrassie (dordogne) et la problème de la définition des néanderthaliens classiques. *L'Anthropologie* 78:6–377.

————. 1989. La nouvelle reconstitution du crane néanderthalien de la Chapelle-aux-Saints: Méthode et résultats. *Bulletin et Mémoires de la Société d'Anthropologie de Paris*, n.s., 1:95–118.

Henke, W. L. 1966. *Dynamic articulatory model of speech production using computer simulation.* Ph.D. diss., MIT.

Hewes, G. W. 1973. Primate communication and the gestural origin of language. *Current Anthropology* 14:5–24.

Holloway, R. L. 1995. Evidence for POT expansion in early *Homo*: A pretty theory with ugly (or no) paleoneurological facts. *Behavioral and Brain Sciences* 18: 191–93.

Houghton, P. 1993. Neanderthal supralaryngeal vocal tract. *American Journal of Physical Anthropology* 90:139–46.

Howells, W. W. 1976. Neanderthal man: Facts and figures. In *Proceedings of the ninth international congress of anthropological and ethnological sciences, Chicago 1973.* The Hague: Mouton.

————. 1989. *Skull shapes and the map: Craniometric analyses in the dispersion of modern Homo.* Papers of the Peabody Museum of Archaeology and Ethnology, vol. 79. Cambridge: Harvard University Press.

Hublin, J.-J., F. Spoor, M. Braun, F. Zonneveld, and S. Condemi. 1996. A late Neanderthal associated with Upper Paleolithic artifacts. *Nature* 381:224–26.

Humbolt, W. von. [1836] 1988. *On language: The diversity of human language-structure and its influence on the mental development of mankind.* Translated by P. Heath. Cambridge: Cambridge University Press.

Itard, J. M. G. 1801. *De l'éducation d'un homme sauvage, ou des premiers développements physiques et moraux du jeune sauvage de l'Averyon.* Paris: Goujon.

Jackendoff, R. 1994. *Patterns in the mind: Language and human nature.* New York: Basic Books.

Jakobson, R. 1940. Kindersprache, Aphasie und allgemeine Lautgesetze. In *Selected Writings.* The Hague: Mouton. Translated by A. R. Keiler. 1968. *Child language, aphasia, and phonological universals.* The Hague: Mouton.

————. 1990. *On Language.* Edited by L R. Waugh and M. Monville-Burston. Cambridge: Harvard University Press.

Jerison, H. J. 1973. *Evolution of the brain and intelligence.* New York: Academic Press.

Just, M. A. , and P. A. Carpenter. 1992. A capacity theory of comprehension: Individual differences in working memory. *Psychological Review* 99:122–49.

Kagan, J., J. S. Reznick, and N. Snidman. 1988. Biological bases of childhood shyness. *Science* 240:167–71.

Kempler, D. 1988. Lexical and pantomime abilities in Alzheimer's disease. *Aphasiology* 2:147–59.

Kempler, D., S. Curtiss, and C. Jackson. 1987. Syntactic preservation in Alzheimer's disease. *Journal of Speech and Hearing Research* 30:343–50.

Kimura, D. 1979. Neuromotor mechanisms in the evolution of human communication. In *Neurobiology of social communication in primates,* ed. H. D. Steklis and M. J Raleith. New York: Academic Press.

Kingdon, J. 1993. *Self-made man.* New York: John Wiley.

Krakauer, J. 1996. Into thin air. *Outside,* September, 46–64, 158–63.

Kratzenstein, C. G. 1780. Sur la formation et la naissance des voyelles. *Observations sur la Physique* 21 (1782): 358–81. Translated from *Acta Academiae Scientiarum Petropolitani.*

Kuhl, P. K. 1981. Discrimination of speech by nonhuman animals: Basic auditory sensitivities conducive to the perception of speech-sound categories. *Journal of the Acoustical Society of America* 70:340–49.

Kuhl, P. K., K. A. Williams, F. Lacerda, K. N. Stevens, and B. Lindblom. 1992. Linguistic experience alters phonetic perception in infants by 6 months of age. *Science* 255:606–8.

Ladefoged, P., and D. E. Broadbent. 1957. Information conveyed by vowels. *Journal of the Acoustical Society of America* 29:98–104.

Ladefoged, P., J. De Clerk, M. Lindau, and G. Papcun. 1972. An auditory-motor theory of speech production. *UCLA Working Papers in Phonetics* 22:48–76.

Laitman, J. T., and R. C. Heimbuch. 1982. The basicranium of Plio-Pleistocene hominids as an indicator of their upper respiratory systems. *American Journal of Physical Anthropology* 59:323–44.

Laitman, J. T., R. C. Heimbuch, and E. S. Crelin. 1978. Developmental changes in a basicranial line and its relationship to the upper respiratory system in living primates. *American Journal of Anatomy* 152:467–82.

———. 1979. The basicranium of fossil hominids as an indicator of their upper respiratory systems. *American Journal of Physical Anthropology* 51:15–34.

Laitman, J. T., and J. S. Reidenberg. 1988. Advances in understanding the relationship between the skull base and larynx with comments on the origins of speech. *Human Evolution* 3:101–11.

Landahl, K. L. 1982. The onset of structural discourse: A developmental study of the acquisition of language. Ph.D. diss., Brown University.

Landahl, K. L., and H. J. Gould. 1986. Congenital malformation of the speech tract in humans and its developmental consequences. In *The biology of change in otolaryngology*, ed. R. J. Ruben, T. R. Van de Water, and E. W. Rubel, 131–49. Amsterdam: Elsevier.

Lange, K. W., T. W. Robbins, C. D. Marsden, M. James, A. M. Owen, and G. M. Paul. 1992. L-dopa withdrawal in Parkinson's disease selectively impairs cognitive performance in tests sensitive to frontal lobe dysfunction. *Psychopharmacology* 107:394–404.

Lattimore, E. 1934. *Turkestan Reunion*. New York: John Day. 1994. Reprint, New York: Kodansha America.

Leakey, M. 1971. *Olduvai Gorge*. Vol. 3, *Excavations in Beds I and II, 1960–1963*. Cambridge: Cambridge University Press.

———. 1995. *New York Times*, November 7, 1995, C6.

Liberman, A. M., F. S. Cooper, D. P. Shankweiler, and M. Studdert-Kennedy. 1967. Perception of the speech code. *Psychological Review* 74:431–61.

Liberman, A. M., and I. G. Mattingly. 1985. The motor theory of speech perception revised. *Cognition* 21:1–36.

Lieberman, D. E., and J. J. Shea. 1994. Behavioral differences between archaic and modern humans in the Levantine Mousterian. *American Anthropologist* 96:300–32.

Lieberman, D. 1995. Testing hypotheses about recent human evolution from skulls. *Current Anthropology* 36:159–98.

Lieberman, D. In press. *The human skull*. Cambridge: Harvard University Press.

Lieberman, M. R., and P. Lieberman. 1973. Olson's "projective verse" and the use of breath control as a structural element. *Language and Style* 5:287–98.

Lieberman, P. 1968. Primate vocalizations and human linguistic ability. *Journal of the Acoustical Society of America* 44:1157–64.

Lieberman, P. 1975. *On the origins of language: An introduction to the evolution of speech*. New York: Macmillan.

———. 1980. On the development of vowel production in young children. In *Child phonology, perception and production*, ed. G. Yeni-Komshian and J. Kavanagh, 113–42. New York: Academic Press.

———. 1984. *The biology and evolution of language*. Cambridge: Harvard University Press.

———. 1985. On the evolution of human syntactic ability: Its pre-adaptive bases—motor control and speech. *Journal of Human Evolution* 14:657–68.

———. 1991. *Uniquely human: The evolution of speech, thought, and selfless behavior*. Cambridge: Harvard University Press.

————. 1994. Hyoid bone position and speech: Reply to Arensburg et al. 1990. *American Journal of Physical Anthropology* 94:275–78.

————. In press. *The functional language system of the human brain.* Cambridge: Harvard University Press.

Lieberman, P., and E. S. Crelin. 1971. On the speech of Neanderthal man. *Linguistic Inquiry* 2:203–22.

Lieberman, P., E. S. Crelin, and D. H. Klatt. 1972. Phonetic ability and related anatomy of the newborn, adult human, Neanderthal man, and the chimpanzee. *American Anthropologist* 74:287–307.

Lieberman, P., J. Friedman, and L. S. Feldman. 1990. Syntactic deficits in Parkinson's disease. *Journal of Nervous and Mental Disease* 178:360–65.

Lieberman, P., E. T. Kako, J. Friedman, G. Tajchman, L. S. Feldman, and E. B. Jiminez. 1992. Speech production, syntax comprehension, and cognitive deficits in Parkinson's disease. *Brain and Language* 43:169–89.

Lieberman, P., B. G. Kanki, A. Protopappas, E. Reed, and J. W. Youngs. 1994. Cognitive defects at altitude. *Nature* 372:325.

Lieberman, P., B. G. Kanki, and A. Protopappas. 1995. Speech production and cognitive decrements on Mount Everest. *Aviation, Space and Environmental Medicine* 66:857–64.

Lieberman, P., and C. -Y. Tseng. 1994. Subcortical pathways essential for speech, language, and cognition: Implications for hominid evolution. *American Journal of Physical Anthropology*, suppl. 16, 93:130.

Lindblom, B. 1988. Models of phonetic variation and selection. In *Language Change and Biological Evolution.* Torino, Italy: Institute for Scientific Interchange.

Lisker, L., and A. S. Abramson. 1964. A cross language study of voicing in initial stops: Acoustical measurements. *Word* 20:384–442.

Lubker, J., and T. Gay. 1982. Anticipatory labial coarticulation: Experimental, biological, and linguistic variables. *Journal of the Acoustical Society of America* 71:437–48.

MacDonald, M. C., N. J. Perlmutter, and M. S. Seidenberg. 1994. Lexical nature of syntactic ambiguity resolution. *Psychological Review* 101:676–703.

MacLean, P. D. 1985. Evolutionary psychiatry and the triune brain. *Psychological Medicine* 15:219–21.

————. 1986. Neurobehavioral significance of the mammal-like reptiles (therapsids). In *The ecology and biology of mammal-like reptiles,* ed. N. Hotton III, J. J. Roth, and E. C. Roth, 1–21. Washington, D.C.: Smithsonian Institution Press.

MacNeill, D. 1985. So you think gestures are nonverbal? *Psychological Review* 92:350–71.

Manley, R. S., and L. C. Braley. 1950. Masticatory performance and efficiency. *Journal of Dental Research* 29:314–21.

Marie, P. 1926. *Travaux et Mémoires* Paris: Masson.

Martin, A., J. V. Haxby, F. M. Lalonde, C. L. Wiggs, and L. G. Ungerleider. 1995. Discrete cortical regions associated with knowledge of color and knowledge of action. *Science* 270:102–5.

Mayr, E. 1982. *The growth of biological thought.* Cambridge: Harvard University Press.

McCarthy, R. C., and D. E. Lieberman. In press. Reconstructing vocal tracts from cranial base flexion: An ontogenetic comparison of cranial base angulation in humans and chimpanzees. *American Journal of Physical Anthropology.*

McGrew, W. C. 1993. The intelligent use of tools: Twenty propositions. In *Tools, language and cognition in human evolution,* ed. K. R. Gibson and T. Ingold, 151–70. Cambridge: Cambridge University Press.

McGurk, H., and J. MacDonald. 1976. Hearing lips and seeing voices. *Nature* 263:747–48.

Mega, M. S., and M. F. Alexander. 1994. Subcortical aphasia: The core profile of capsulostriatal infarction. *Neurology* 44:1824–29.

Mellars, P. 1996. *The Neanderthal legacy: An archaeological perspective from western Europe.* Princeton: Princeton University Press.

Mesulam, M. -M. 1990. Large-scale neurocognitive networks and distributed processing for attention, language, and memory. *Annals of Neurology* 28:597–613.

Metter, E. J., D. Kempler, C. A. Jackson, W. R. Hanson, W. H. Riege, L. M. Camras, J.C. Mazziotta, and M. E. Phelps. 1987. Cerebular glucose metabolism in chronic aphasia. *Neurology* 37:1599–606.

Metter, E. J., W. H. Riege, W. R. Hanson M. E. Phelps, and D. E. Kuhl. 1984. Local cerebral metabolic rates of glucose in movement and language disorders from positron tomography. *American Journal of Physiology* 246:R897–R900.

Mishra, S., T. R. Venkatesan, S. N. Rajaguru, and B. L. K. Somayajulu. 1995. Earliest Acheulian industry from peninsular India. *Current Anthropology* 36:847–51.

Müller, J. 1848. *The physiology of the senses, voice and muscular motion with the mental faculties.* Translated by W. Baly. London: Walton and Maberly.

Natsopoulos, D., G. Grouios, S. Bostantzopoulou, G. Mentenopoulos, Z. Katsarou, and J. Logothetis. 1994. Algorithmic and heuristic strategies in comprehension of complement clauses by patients with Parkinson's disease. *Neuropsychologia* 31:951–64.

Negus, V. E. 1949. *The comparative anatomy and physiology of the larynx.* New York: Hafner.

Parent, A. 1986. *Comparative neurobiology of the basal ganglia.* New York: John Wiley.

Peterson, G. E., and H. L. Barney. 1952. Control methods used in a study of the vowels. *Journal of the Acoustical Society of America* 24:175–84.

Pinker, S. 1994. *The language instinct: How the mind creates language.* New York: William Morrow.

Pinker, S., and P. Bloom. 1990. Natural selection and natural language. *Behavioral and Brain Sciences* 13:707–84.

Protopappas, A., and P. Lieberman. In press. Fundamental frequency of phonation and perceived emotional stress. *Journal of the Acoustical Society of America.*

Rauschecker, J. P., and Korte, M. 1993. Auditory compensation for early blindness in cat cerebral cortex. *Journal of Neuroscience* 18:4538–48.

Roberts, C. J., and C. R. Lowe. 1975. Where have all the conceptions gone? *Lancet* 1:498–99.

Ruhlen, M. 1994. *On the origin of language: Tracing the evolution of the mother tongue.* New York: John Wiley.

Rumbaugh, D. M., and E. S. Savage-Rumbaugh. 1992. Biobehavioral roots of language: Words, apes and a child. Conference paper presented at University of Bielefeld, Germany.

Rumelhart, D. E., J. L. McClelland, and the PDP Research Group. 1986. *Parallel distributed processing: Explorations in the microstructures of cognition.* Vol. 1. Cambridge: MIT Press.

Sachs, J., P. Lieberman, and D. Erikson. 1972. Anatomical and cultural determinants of male and female speech. In *Language attitudes: Current trends and prospects.* Monograph no. 25. Washington, D.C.: Georgetown University.

Saffran, J. R., R. N. Aslin, and E. L. Newport. 1996. Statistical learning by 8-month-old infants. *Science* 274:1926–28.

Savage-Rumbaugh, E. S., and Rumbaugh, D. 1993. The emergence of language. In *Tools, language and cognition in human evolution,* ed. K. R. Gibson and T. Ingold. 86–100. Cambridge: Cambridge University Press.

Seebach, B. S., N. Intrator, P. Lieberman, and L. N. Cooper. 1994. A model of prenatal acquisition of speech parameters. *Proceedings of National Academy of Sciences, USA* 91:7473–76.

Sereno, J., and P. Lieberman. 1987. Developmental aspects of lingual coarticulation. *Journal of Phonetics* 15:247–57.

Singleton. J. L., and E. L. Newport. N.d. When learners surpass their models: The acquisition of American Sign Language from impoverished input. Unpublished MS.

Slotnick, B. M. 1967. Disturbances of maternal behavior in the rat following lesions of the cingulate cortex. *Behavior* 24:204–36.

Sokoloff, A. J. 1989. The organization of the hyoglossal nucleus: An experimental neuroanatomical investigation of hyoglossal-lingual and cortico-hyoglossal projections in *Macaca fasicularis* and other vertebrate species. Ph.D. diss., Harvard University.

Solecki, R. S. 1971. *Shanidar, the first flower people.* New York: Knopf.

Stephan, H., H. Frahm, and G. Baron. 1981. New and revised data on volumes of brain structures in insectivores and primates. *Folia Primatologia* 35:1–29.

Stevens, K. N. 1972. Quantal nature of speech. In *Human communication: A unified view,* ed. E. E. David, Jr., and P. D. Denes, chap. 3. New York: McGraw-Hill.

Stevens, K. N., and A. S. House. 1955. Development of a quantitative description of vowel articulation. *Journal of the Acoustical Society of America* 27:484–93.

Stringer, C. B. 1992. Evolution of early humans. In *The Cambridge encyclopedia of human evolution,* ed. S. Jones, R. Martin, and D. Pilbeam, 241–51. Cambridge: Cambridge University Press.

Stringer, C. B., and P. Andrews. 1988. Genetic and fossil evidence for the origin of modern humans. *Science* 239:1263–68.

Stromswold, K., D. Caplan, N. Alpert, and S. Rausch. 1996. Localization of syntactic processing by positron emission tomography. *Brain and Language* 51:452–73.

Susman, R. L. 1994. Fossil evidence for early hominid tool use. *Science* 265:1570–73.

Terrace, H. S., L. A. Petitto, R. J. Sanders, and T. G. Bever. 1979. Can an ape create a sentence? *Science* 206:891–902.

Toth, N., and K. Schick. 1993. Early stone industries. In *Tools, language and cognition in human evolution,* ed. K. R. Gibson and T. Ingold, 346–62. Cambridge: Cambridge University Press.

Truby, H. L., J. F. Bosma, and J. Lind. 1965. *Newborn infant cry.* Upsalla: Almquist and Wiksell.

Vargha-Khadem, F., K. Watkins, R. Passingham, and P. Fletcher. 1995. Cognitive and praxic deficits in a large family with a genetically transmitted speech and language disorder. *Proceedings of the National Academy of Sciences* 92:930–33.

Wernicke, C. 1874. Der aphasische Symptomencomplex: Eine psychologische Studie auf anatomischer Basis. Breslau: Cohn and Weigert. Translated 1969. In *Boston studies in the philosophy of science,* vol 4, ed. R. S. Cohen and M. W. Wartofsky, 34–97. Boston: Reidel.

Wilkins, W. K., and J. Wakefield. 1995. Brain evolution and neurolinguistic preconditions. *Behavioral and Brain Sciences* 18:161–226.

Wood, B. A. 1992. Evolution of australopithecines. In *The Cambridge encyclopedia of human evolution*, ed. S. Jones, R. Martin, and D. Pilbeam, 231–40. Cambridge: Cambridge University Press.

Wright, R. 1994. *The moral animal*. New York: Random House.

Zubrow, E. 1990. The demographic modelling of Neanderthal extinction. In *The human revolution: Behavioral and biological perspectives on the origin of modern humans*. Vol. 1. Edited by P. Mellars and C. B. Stringer, 212–31. Edinburgh: Edinburgh University Press.

Index

1, 4, 17, 28, 31 32 33 34 40 41 42 44 45 46 69 70 78 84
105, 106 121 72 130, 137 147